THE JAPANESE GRILL

THE JAPANESE GRILL

FROM CLASSIC YAKITORI TO STEAK, SEAFOOD, AND VEGETABLES

Tadashi Ono & Harris Salat

Food photography by Todd Coleman | Location photography by Jun Takagi

TEN SPEED PRESS
Berkeley

Copyright © 2011 by Tadashi Ono and Harris Salat
Food photographs copyright © 2011 by Todd Coleman
Location photographs copyright © 2011 by Jun Takagi

Published in the United States by Ten Speed Press,
an imprint of the Crown Publishing Group,
a division of Random House, Inc., New York.
www.crownpublishing.com
www.tenspeed.com

Ten Speed Press and the Ten Speed Press colophon are
registered trademarks of Random House, Inc.

Library of Congress Cataloging-in-Publication Data
Ono, Tadashi, 1962-
The Japanese grill: from classic yakitori to steak, seafood, and vegetables /
by Tadashi Ono, Harris Salat.—1st ed.
      p. cm.
Includes index.
Summary: "A full-color cookbook that introduces American palates to
authentic Japanese-style grilling, with recipes that skillfully blend traditional
ingredients and modern twists to create remarkable meals"—Provided by
publisher.
1. Cooking, Japanese. 2. Cookbooks. I. Salat, Harris. II. Title.
TX724.5.J3O56 2011
641.5952—dc22

                        2010045869

ISBN 978-1-58008-737-7
Printed in China

Cover and text design by Toni Tajima

American-style grills provided by Weber

10 9 8 7 6 5 4 3 2 1
First Edition

641.5952

CONTENTS

ACKNOWLEDGMENTS

TADASHI: I'd like to thank my wonderful, grill-loving family—my wife Manami and daughters Sueh and Kiku—for all the fantastic backyard barbecues we've shared. They're my inspiration for this book. I'd also like to thank Sean McPherson, Eric Goode, Mikio Shinagawa, Richard Born and Ira Driker, the owners of Matsuri restaurant, for their support; Maurice Rodrigues of the Maritime Hotel; and Taka Terashita and the rest of the crew in the Matsuri kitchen.

HARRIS: I'd like to thank my lovely wife, Momoyo, for her support and impeccable taste buds. And I want to remember my late dad, Sol, who discovered grilling when he immigrated to America, and made it a summertime fixture for our family when I was growing up—thanks, dad, for instilling in me a love for anything grilled.

BOTH OF US: In no particular order, we'd like to thank the amazing team at Ten Speed Press; the good folks at Weber-Stephen Products Co. for their incredible grills and generous support; our rockin' volunteer recipe testers from around the world; the gang at *Saveur* magazine for all their assistance and for lending us their props; Mr. Kosei Yamamoto and the staff of Mutual Trading Co.; our pals and photographers Todd Coleman and Jun Takagi; Ms. Saori Kawano and Korin Trading Co.; Staubitz Market, New York's best butcher; Chef Yoshihiro Murata of Kikunoi restaurant in Kyoto; and our stellar researchers, Chisato Uno and Jamie Graves.

INTRODUCTION

WELCOME TO OUR second Japanese cookbook, one we're incredibly excited about. The first, *Japanese Hot Pots*, introduced traditional one-pot cooking to America: warm, comforting, soupy dishes, the perfect balm for a frigid winter's day. Now we're turning our attention to grilling, the quintessential fare for sunny weather. Like our first book, this one was conceived during a leisurely meal at Tadashi's house. Make that a wiffle-ball game-*cum*-grilling extravaganza in his backyard. While family and friends took turns at bat with his young daughters, Tadashi manned the grill, cooking up miso-marinated steaks; veggies basted with lemon and soy sauce; simply salted whole sea bass; spicy, citrusy lamb chops; corn on the cob slathered with butter and soy sauce. Tadashi's kettle grill proclaimed "America," but the mouthwatering, mind-blowing flavors coming off the charcoal-fueled fire unmistakably trumpeted "Japan." We had a *eureka* moment. This book followed not too long after.

ROOTS OF JAPANESE GRILLING

Throughout humanity, sizzling food over fire has been about as fundamental a cooking technique as it gets. Since ancient times in Japan, the nexus of a traditional home has been the *irori*, or open hearth, a square fire pit sunk into the floor. The *irori* is where people gathered, their sitting positions dictated by hierarchy and tradition. The *irori* provided light and heat for the home. The *irori* dried clothes, wood, and food for preservation. And the *irori* is where families cooked, suspending a pot over the fire; burying foods and bottles of sake in the ashes to heat them; and grilling fish, skewered and staked upright to face the fire.

Yakimono, literally "grilled things" in reference to food, is a centerpiece of Japanese cooking, one of the primary courses that comprise the intensely seasonal and profoundly sublime *kaiseki* meal, the highest expression of the cuisine. But grilling isn't just for rarified eating. Unlike in the West, Japanese have traditionally cooked without an oven, relying instead on fire to caramelize and roast foods. Even today, a classic Japanese breakfast includes miso soup, pickles, a bowl of rice, and piece of grilled fish, even if that fish was grilled on a stovetop contraption in the home. Grilling plays a central role not only in family cooking, but also in the soul food Japanese crave when they go out, including yakitori (page 19); *robata*, a rustic style of grilling that evokes the ancient *irori*; and the grilled dishes that make up the tapas-like plates of *izakaya* (eating pub) dining.

Tadashi grew up in Tokyo, where people satisfied their yen for grilled foods in restaurants. Most homes in Japan, especially in the cities, don't have backyards. Instead, his neighborhood was itself a grilling haven, full of yakitori and *yakiton* (grilled pork) joints, mom-and-pop places that specialized in skewered chicken and pork grilled over glowing charcoal, as well as restaurants offering delicate slices of grilled wagyu beef (see "Wagyu," page 102) and pristine roasted fish. These places infused meat, poultry, and fish with traditional Japanese seasonings like soy sauce; mirin; miso; sake; and a fiery, citrusy condiment called *yuzu kosho* to create incredibly delicious dishes.

AMERICAN GRILLING, JAPANESE FLAVORS

So here we were, a Japanese-born chef and an American food writer hooked on Japanese food and culture, sharing a bountiful meal with Japanese flavors prepared on that icon of American casual cooking—a Weber kettle grill. Can the Japanese devotion to grilling translate to our American way of cooking and eating? As we happily devoured Tadashi's parade of grilled dishes, we were struck by a couple of things. First, we realized how much we love the red-white-and-blue Amer-

ican kind of grilling and how important it is to us. Tadashi discovered this style of grilling when he arrived in America from Japan twenty-five years ago and has been a devoted fan since. Harris, the son of immigrants, grew up with the backyard grill, his dad an avid griller from the moment he came to our shores. For both of us, grilling wasn't just a way to cook—it was a way to be American.

We also were amazed how well Japanese flavors worked with grilled foods beyond traditional Japanese dishes. While classic Japanese grilling means skewers or thin slices of beef (Japan is a chopstick culture, after all, so no knife and fork), Tadashi's brainstorm was to apply these same great flavors to the steaks, burgers, chops, whole chickens, and other chunks of irresistible flesh, as well as delectable veggies, that we love to grill here in America.

Meat in Japanese Cooking

Eating meat has been central to traditional diets across the globe, from beef in Europe to pork in China, but not so in Japan. Starting around the year 675 A.D., the Japanese emperor began prohibiting the consumption of meat on religious grounds; both Buddhism and Shintoism, the two major religions, had injunctions against killing living creatures. The ban started with the clergy, then spread to the general population, who avoided most animals (seafood was allowed and didn't fall under the taboo). Hunters deep in the countryside, though, continued to bag game (boar was euphemistically called "mountain whale," perhaps to make it more palatable), and certain "medicine eating" of meat was accepted. All this changed in the mid-nineteenth century, when Japan reopened to the world after 300 years of isolation. Westerners arrived, with their Western ideas about meat—which was, basically, unless you ate it, you'd be a ninety-pound weakling for life. The Japanese military soon incorporated meat into soldiers' diet to treat the wounded and feed the navy, and restaurants specializing in meat (interestingly, chicken was more prized than beef at the time) started popping up. Enjoying meat was considered modern eating, and its popularity spread quickly.

UMAMI

For much of Japan's history, eating meat was taboo (see "Meat in Japanese Cooking," page 2), so Japanese cooks intuitively developed ways to infuse a satisfying, meat-like savoriness to foods, but without the meat. The key reason why traditional Japanese seasonings make food so yummy is because they're fermented, a process that naturally releases profound flavor compounds in ingredients (see "The Power of Fermented Japanese Ingredients," page 8). Those compounds are what's called umami. You might not be familiar with the word, but you already know the taste. You sense it whenever you bite into a chunk of fine Parmesan, a perfectly ripe heirloom tomato, or a sizzling porterhouse; it's that almost indescribable mouthwatering savoriness that beckons you to eat more. And when these flavors meet fire, they create an even greater taste explosion, with the natural goodness of meat, poultry, fish, or veggies marrying with the umami intrinsic to the seasonings and the God-it's-making-me-salivate caramelization and char. Umami, rather than the butter or acidic vinegar used in Western cooking, is the secret flavor weapon here. Now think how much more incredible a piece of already amazing meat will taste enhanced with natural seasonings bursting with this meat-like savoriness. That's the idea behind the Japanese grill.

OUR SIMPLE AND INCREDIBLY DELICIOUS APPROACH TO GRILLING

The dishes in our book are a collection of traditional Japanese grilling techniques, like authentic yakitori, *shioyaki* (salt grilling), and other favorites, as well as contemporary recipes tuned to the way we grill in America. Big juicy steaks, pork chops, whole chickens, and American-style fillets of fish aren't typical eating in Japan, but, as Tadashi discovered early on, taste fantastic with Japanese flavors. The marinades in our book, we think, pair perfectly with the main ingredients in the recipes. But you can also try them with other ingredients if you'd like; they're all simple; fast-marinating; and very, very flexible. You'll see, too, that our contemporary marinades often marry traditional Japanese seasonings with oil. This creates even more benefits—oil adds moisture and juiciness to ingredients, helps ingredients brown, and binds the seasonings.

When it's time to grill, for many of our recipes we apply the classic yakitori grilling technique to other dishes: We grill meat partway, brush on marinade, then continue grilling, which caramelizes the marinade on the meat. This fundamental method for sizzling yakitori works perfectly with chicken, fish, or meat—the inside of the meat cooks exactly right, while the marinade browns to a fragrant, glossy nirvana. When you try, say, one of our steak or swordfish dishes using this simple method, the results will amaze you. Chapter One, page 19, is all about yakitori grilling.

Whether you grill on charcoal or gas, crave salt-crusted shrimp, sizzled shiitake mushrooms, or a thick, juicy, charred sirloin, we know you'll love the recipes in our book. So light the coals or flip on the gas and discover the pleasures and delights of the Japanese grill.

Planning a Japanese Grill Meal

If you're feeding a group, plan on at least five different dishes. Mix and match main ingredients (meat, poultry, fish, veggies), vary the marinades and sauces (based on, for instance, soy sauce, miso, or fiery *yuzu kosho*), and include at least a couple of our side dishes. Besides being delicious and a snap to prepare, the side dishes' bright, light, and vinegary flavors serve as a counterweight to all that rich, roasted protein. Finally, one or two *yaki onigiri*—grilled rice balls (page 155)—will add a tasty dose of carbs to round out the meal. Wholesome, balanced eating without fretting about it.

Itadakimasu!—Bon appétit, as they say in Japan.

THE BASICS: JAPANESE INGREDIENTS

ESSENTIAL INGREDIENTS

These are the fundamental ingredients that create the mouthwatering flavors of Japanese grilling. "Sources" (page 181) offers stores and websites that carry them. To help you track down what you need, "Finding Ingredients" (page 184) lists ingredients in both English and Japanese.

Soy sauce Fermented from soybeans and wheat, soy sauce adds character, umami-driven savoriness, and caramel flavor and color to foods. We prefer Japanese soy sauce over Chinese or other types because it is more subtle and not as strongly fermented. For the recipes in this book, stick to the all-purpose, standard Japanese soy sauce (*koikuchi*), readily available at Asian and Japanese markets.

Sake This quintessential Japanese alcoholic drink is also a fundamental cooking ingredient. Brewed through a process that's closer to brewing beer than making wine (calling it "rice wine" is a misnomer), sake is produced from special rice that's been polished to remove the outer layer, keeping the starchy kernel intact. Sake adds sweetness, acidity, and depth to foods and is crucial for diminishing the sense of fishiness in fish (see "Forget Fishiness," page 68). Don't use so-called cooking sake; buy the actual brew. Any basic (and we mean inexpensive) sake works great for our recipes.

Mirin Brewed from glutinous rice, mirin is a sweet cooking liquid more nuanced than plain sugar. Mirin adds depth and umami-rich flavor as well as a shiny glaze to foods (which makes it great for grilling). Sometimes confusingly called "sweet sake," mirin is not sake, but does contain alcohol. For dipping sauce recipes, we boil mirin first to evaporate the alcohol, but in marinades, use as is. Use an artisan-made mirin if you can find one (most versions you'll come across here are industrially produced).

Miso A paste fermented from soybeans and salt, or soybeans, salt, and rice or barley, this classic staple comes in hundreds of varieties. Miso is a concentrated source of protein and a live, cultured substance like yogurt with lactic acid–forming bacteria that aids digestion. In cooking, it adds savory, robust, umami-laden flavor to foods. Look for miso with just the primary ingredients, no additives. Varieties range in taste from lightly sweet to deeply savory. In this book we use the four kinds described here.

- *Shiro miso* (white miso) is a salty, rice-based miso, in colors that range from straw to yellow ocher. Look for *Shinshu shiro* (*Shinshu* white), a versatile variety from the Japanese Alps, or use another salty, rice-based white variety.
- *Aka miso* (red miso) is a salty, rice-based miso that's aged longer than white, resulting in a deeper, more savory flavor and a reddish color. Look for *Sendai* miso, a coarsely ground, rustic variety (a favorite); *Shinshu aka* (Shinshu red); or another rice-based red miso.

- *Hatcho miso* is a dense, chocolate-hued paste with an intense, meaty savoriness. Fermented from soybeans and salt in huge cedar barrels for two years, powerful *Hatcho* pairs perfectly with meat. You can also use *aka dashi*, which is *Hatcho* cut with *saikyo* miso and is sometimes easier to find.
- *Saikyo miso* is lightly fermented with the highest proportion of rice of any miso, which gives it its trademark delicately sweet flavor. The signature, cream-colored miso of Kyoto, *Saikyo* is very refined, with a smooth, silky texture.

Yuzu kosho This zesty condiment is the perfect companion to grilled foods and one of our favorite Japanese ingredients. An alluring, aromatic marriage of fiery chilies, salt, and tangy Japanese yuzu citrus zest and juice, *yuzu kosho* comes in two styles: red, with a more rounded flavor, and the sharper green. Both add palate-popping flavor and heat to meat, chicken, and fish. We use a ton of it in the book. You can find *yuzu kosho* at Japanese markets and on Amazon (search for "yuzu kosho").

Japanese sea salt We love this traditional salt, called *arajio* and available in Japanese markets. Salt crystals don't form on land in Japan, so have long been extracted there from the sea. This coarse salt is still damp with brine and brimming with complex mineral and ocean flavors. It's quite potent, so be careful not to oversalt. You can also dry *Arajio* to make it easier to sprinkle, if you'd like: spread the crystals on a sheet pan and bake at 400°F for 10 minutes. Cool before using.

Oils We use a trio of oils in the book: vegetable, sesame, and olive. Sesame oil is a traditional Japanese ingredient that adds flavor and incredible aroma to grilled dishes. Use only roasted sesame oil (oil from raw sesame seed is also available in Japanese stores). Olive oil, a contemporary ingredient now widely used in Japan, does the same thing in its own way. For vegetable oil, any good variety works, like peanut or a blend.

Tobanjan This red paste is fermented from soybeans and chilies and was originally a Chinese culinary import to Japan. *Tobanjan* adds potent heat and its own fermented flavor; be careful not add too much, or it can overwhelm other foods.

CLASSIC ACCENTS

These spices, seasonings, and ingredients add sublime dimension to grilled dishes. We use them to spike dipping sauces, marinades, and dressings or to add a final flourish to tantalize the palate.

Wasabi The fragrance, clean flavor, and subtle heat of this classic Japanese ingredient enliven the palate like nothing else. A rhizome with lime-colored flesh, fresh wasabi is expensive and hard to find here. But if you can get it, grate with a fine grater. Alternatives are pure wasabi paste in a tube or an economical wasabi-flavored mixture sold in a tube or as a powder.

Sansho A relative of the Chinese Sichuan pepper (both not true peppers), this ground spice gives off an intense citrusy fragrance and is more aromatic than hot. We typically use *sansho* (sometimes spelled *sansyo*) to accent rich foods to balance their fattiness.

Shichimi togarashi A versatile, popular Japanese spice that originated in the 1600s, it's made from a mixture of seven ingredients. Ground chili is the main component, to which *sansho*, sesame seed, and other aromatics like yuzu citrus peel, mustard seed, hemp seed, and poppy seed are added. Sometimes called *nanami togarashi*, it is distinct from *ichimi togarashi*, which is pure ground chili.

Ume **paste** This red paste is made from *umeboshi*, salt-pickled Japanese apricots (sometimes mistakenly referred to as salt-pickled plums), and adds bright, tart, and salty notes that titillate the palate. It's usually sold in jars and sometimes called *umeboshi* paste.

Karashi **mustard** Ground from a blend of pure mustard seeds, *karashi* isn't cut with vinegar like Western mustards. As a result, it's sinus-clearing hot. You'll find it as a paste in a tube or as a powder. For the powder, add hot water to work into a thick paste, and wait a minute or two to use. *Karashi* is sometimes called "Japanese hot mustard" or "Japanese mustard."

Shiso A member of the mint family, the heart-shaped leaves of this tender, fragrant herb have distinctive sawtooth edges. There are two kinds of shiso—purple and green, with the green variety (also called *ohba*) commonly available here. Discard the stems and use only the leaves in dishes.

Garlic For most marinades in this book, process garlic by grating, rather than chopping or passing through a garlic press. This is important, because grating breaks down the cells to create much more fragrant garlicky heat, which is what you want in a marinade. Use a fine grater or a rasp-type tool if you have one.

Ginger Fresh ginger brightens the palate and also plays an important role in balancing and diminishing the sense of "fishiness" in fish.

Sesame seed Use only roasted sesame seed for our dishes. Sesame seed comes in two varieties—black and white. We usually call for white, but feel free to mix types, if you'd like.

Yukari **shiso salt** This accent is made from powdered, dried purple shiso leaves mixed with salt and adds tangy, salty flavor. It can be referred to in stores as a kind of *furikake*, a topping sprinkled on hot rice. This accent is also sold as *"yukari,"* "shiso *yukari,"* "shiso *furikake,"* or *"yukari* shiso rice seasoning."

ume paste

aka miso

saikyo miso

hatcho miso

shiro miso

green yuzu kosho

柚子こしょう

YUZU KOSHŌ

shiso

tobanjan

red yuzu kosho

arajio (sea salt)

S&B SANSYO JAPANESE PEPPER NET WT. 12g 0.42 OZ.

wasabi powder

sansho

shichimi togarashi

yukari

mitsuba

karashi mustard

THE BASICS: GRILLING

SETTING UP YOUR GRILL

What kind of grill should you use, charcoal or gas? It boils down to heat and convenience. Which is best for you? A totally personal choice. Tadashi, who grills for his family almost every Sunday, three seasons a year, insists on charcoal for its purity of cooking and flavor. Harris also loves charcoal, but keeps a gas grill handy for hurry-up weeknight grilling. For this book, we stick to the two most popular grilling options for our recipes, kettle-style charcoal grills and gas grills, and base our timings on them.

Charcoal grills Not only do charcoal grills pump out a lot more heat than gas grills, they also surround foods with enveloping rays from the glowing coals, searing and cooking foods in a way gas grills just can't. And besides the high temperatures, charcoal, especially lump charcoal, produces a singular smoky flavor. With charcoal grills, though, you have to start a fire, maintain it, manage temperature, and clean up the ash. It's more work, but the challenge makes the results that much more rewarding.

Gas grills No doubt about it, gas grills are much more convenient to use than charcoal grills and easier to control, and there's no messy ash to trash after dinner. And gas grills like the Weber we used in our book have special metal bars that vaporize dripping juices, thus adding flavor while eliminating flare-ups.

Kamado grills We also want to mention charcoal-fueled kamado-style grills like the Big Green Egg. These are grills lined with high-fire ceramics or other types of earthenware that do a great job of retaining heat, so you can grill much hotter. They have a cultish following; as fans can attest, foods grilled on them turn out fantastic. If you do use an Egg or any other kamado-style grill for the recipes in this book, follow its user's guide to adjust recipe timing.

Charcoal When grilling with charcoal, a good-quality lump hardwood charcoal is best. These irregularly shaped chunks of natural charcoal are 100 percent hardwood and contain no additives. They burn hotter and faster than charcoal briquettes, so cook foods better. Lump charcoal is more expensive than briquettes, but if it fits your budget, go with it. Otherwise, look for all-natural charcoal briquettes, which are not laced with additives like regular briquettes.

Chimney starter With any type of charcoal, light the briquettes with a cylindrical chimney starter rather than lighter fuel, which infuses food with an unappealing, fuel-tinged flavor. You'll find them at any store that sells grilling equipment. *To use:* Pile charcoal into the top chamber and stuff crumpled newspaper into the bottom chamber, which has holes on the sides. Set the chimney starter on the lower grate of your grill (which holds the charcoal) and light the newspaper. The coals will ignite; when they're covered with gray ash, they're ready for cooking. (Chimney starters get very hot and must

Japanese Grills

Kettle and gas grills rule the American backyard. But Japanese use different kinds of grills that are also terrific and available here. First, let's dispel a myth: In Japan, hibachi aren't grills. There, they are cylindrical or box-shaped containers (earthenware or earthenware-lined) used for smoldering charcoal to heat a room. Somehow, in America, the word *hibachi* came to mean a small-sized grill or a flat-top griddle. Small Japanese grills are actually called *shichirin*. These grills are made from earthenware or ceramics; come in different sizes; and are cylindrical, square, or rectangular. Some are small enough to rest on a tabletop, which you see in restaurants in Japan. Charcoal-fired *konro* are larger grills, typically rectangular shaped, and made from heat-proof ceramics or metal. These are the grills used at yakitori joints to sizzle perfect skewers of chicken; their narrow fireboxes concentrate and focus heat from the charcoal while at the same time insulating the hands that turn the skewers. *Konro* are perfect for Japanese skewer grilling (page 19) but also typically come with removable wire-mesh cooking grates, so you can use those as well. *Konro* are sold in various sizes; a 54-centimeter version (about 21 inches) is perfect for home use, and, as we can personally attest, an incredible way to grill foods (see "Sources," page 177 , for retailers). With all these Japanese grills, you don't use typical American charcoal, lump or not. Instead, you burn binchotan, an almost magical, artisan-made Japanese charcoal (see "Binchotan," page 12).

be handled safely. Be sure to fully read the user's guide that accompanies this tool before the first use.)

INDISPENSABLE TOOLS

No matter how kitted-out your charcoal or gas set-up, you need the right tools to grill successfully. You don't need a ton of stuff, just these indispensable tools:

Grill brush A heavy duty, steel-bristled brush will let you scrape off the gunk that accumulates on your cooking grate. Use it before and after you grill so foods won't stick. Preheat the grill, then brush the cooking grate like you mean it.

Oil wad This one's a DIY (do-it-yourself) tool—either a wad of paper towels or an old kitchen towel. It works in tandem with the grill brush to ensure that food won't stick. Dunk the wadded paper or towel in a small container of vegetable oil ($1/2$ cup is fine). Preheat the grill, then scrape the cooking grate with your grill brush. Now grab the oil-soaked wad with tongs and completely coat the cooking grate with oil. It might get a little smoky when you oil the grate, but don't worry, that will dissipate quickly.

Tongs Buy a pair of sturdy, 16-inch-long steel tongs to safely turn foods on the grill without burning yourself (and also do the oil-wad trick described before). Use tongs, not a monster fork, to turn foods; you don't want to pierce your precious (and expensive) steak or chop and let all its luscious juices run out.

Kitchen chopsticks Called *saibashi* in Japanese, these super-sized kitchen chopsticks (14 inches long and up) are incredibly handy for turning delicate or small ingredients on the grill—scallops or spears of asparagus, for example. You can

lump charcoal

binchotan

briquettes

Binchotan

Made from the branches of Japanese oak, *binchotan* is a revered, traditional white charcoal. While the word dates back to the 1700s, charcoal-making in Japan reaches back over a millennium and has played a central role in Japanese cooking since. What makes *binchotan* so special? Produced by artisans following the laborious methods handed down through the generations, the oak is fired in an earthen kiln for about a week, producing charcoal so hard it clinks like glass when struck together. *Binchotan*, which still keeps the natural shape of the branches from which it's derived, burns for hours, smokeless and odorless, at a whopping 1,800°F. It's an integral element of *chanoyu*, the Japanese way of tea, where it's used for ritualistically heating the water. It is also essential for Japanese grilling because the very action of its intense infrared rays creates umami flavor compounds in ingredients—so just grilling something on *binchotan* makes it taste better. The best *binchotan* comes from one tiny area in Japan, the Kishu region of Wakayama Prefecture, and is expensive; only certain oak of a certain age can be used, and few charcoal artisans plying this trade remain. But pricy or not, *binchotan* is the charcoal of choice for chefs devoted to grilling. Because it's so hard, lighting *binchotan* is tough; you have to place it over a live fire to ignite it. Once lit, it often takes an hour or more for the charcoal to become coated with white ash and reach cooking temperature. But because it burns so long, you can *very* carefully transfer red-hot *binchotan* from a grill to a *hikeshi tsubo* (fire-extinguishing pot), a special earthenware jar that will hold and eventually extinguish the charcoal, so you can use it again and again, until it reduces to dust.

find these inexpensive wood or bamboo chopsticks at Japanese food markets.

Spatula A spatula is critical for flipping fish fillets, burgers, or any other delicate foods that can break apart on the grill. Use a spatula with a blade at least 6 inches long. An all-metal spatula, the kind that does yeoman's work on the kitchen stove, is great. If you're grilling fish fillets, keep two handy, which makes turning easier.

Basting brush We baste like nobody's business in this book, so a sturdy basting brush is a must. The best choice is a natural boar-bristle brush with a long handle that will keep your hand safely away from the heat. Make sure to hand-wash these brushes in hot, soapy water after each use. Avoid nylon bristles as they can melt if they touch the grate. An alternative is a brush with silicone bristles, as silicone can withstand higher temperatures.

Spray bottle Keep a water-filled spray bottle handy to kill flare-ups before they scorch and blacken your food.

Hand fan Use a sturdy hand fan or paddle fan two ways: to fan coals when you start your fire so they reach grilling temperature quicker and to fan coals when they're losing power, to revive them with a blast of oxygen-rich air.

Flare-Ups

When fat drips from foods and hits red-hot coals, the fat smokes—then flares. These mini-fires can spell disaster for the grill, coating ingredients with black soot or scorching them beyond repair. A cover helps fight flare-ups by cutting off oxygen; otherwise use these two methods: First, leave enough room on the grill to shift foods. As soon as there's a flare-up, move an ingredient to another part of the grill while the flare-up burns out. Another option is to spray down those flames with a water-filled spray bottle. (You can do both options concurrently, of course.) Either way, you want to grill on coals, not shooting flames, so tamp down flare-ups right away.

Grill Marks

The gorgeous crosshatched grill marks that you see on the meat, chicken, and fish photographed for this book were created by Tadashi, who did the grilling for the pictures, and who is a pro chef. But with a little practice, home cooks can also sear these distinctive marks on the foods they prepare. Here's how: Sear your ingredient for about 1 minute. Now, without flipping, give the ingredient a quarter turn (so it shifts 90 degrees). When it's time to flip the ingredient , repeat this process on the other side. Grill marks aren't a must, but they do make foods look pretty—and mouthwatering.

MANAGING HEAT

Managing heat on a stovetop is easy: just adjust the burner's controls this way or that and choose cookware like copper or cast iron to improve heat retention. Managing heat on the grill, on the other hand, is a whole different ballgame. On the grill, of course, you're dealing with direct flames, so you have to know how to do two things. First, you have to gauge temperature using either "hand over fire" technique or a grilling temperature (see "Temperature Chart," below). And second, depending on the recipe, we grill one of three ways: direct, two-zone, or indirect.

Temperature Chart

In the book we specify the optimal temperature level for grilling specific foods, ranging from "hot" to "low." This chart gives the approximate temperature readings for each level and a quick test to estimate it—by gauging how many seconds you can hold your hand above the fire. A grill thermometer, which sits directly on the cooking grate, can come in handy, too.

HEAT LEVEL	APPROXIMATE TEMPERATURE	SECONDS YOU CAN HOLD YOUR HAND 6 INCHES ABOVE THE FIRE
Hot	550°F	2 seconds
Medium-hot	450°F	3 to 4 seconds
Medium	400°F	5 to 6 seconds
Medium-low	350°F	7 seconds
Low	300°F	8 seconds

Direct grilling This is the default grilling method in the book. Food is cooked directly over coals at the temperature level specified in the recipe. Most direct grilling is done uncovered, but for thick cuts like steaks we grill direct and use the cover, too, which speeds up cooking, prevents flare-ups, and heats more evenly.

Two-zone grilling For this method, we set up two temperature levels inside the grill—a hotter area to sear foods and one that is less hot to cook the foods through without burning them. For a charcoal grill, mound half the coals on half of the grill to create the hotter cooking area and arrange the remaining coals in an even layer on the other half to establish the lower-temperature cooking area. For a gas grill, adjust the temperature on two burners. Our recipes dictate which two temperature levels to use, usually hot and medium.

Indirect grilling We use this method to slow-grill some thick cuts over low heat for a long time and for smoking. For a charcoal grill, pile the charcoal on one half of the grill only; leave the other half empty. Fill an aluminum tray with water and place it on the empty side of the lower grate (this will add humidity, cool the fire, and catch drips). For a gas grill, fire one burner, leave the other one turned off, and place the tray of water over it. For both charcoal and gas grills, food is placed on the empty side and cooked by the heat produced from the adjacent hot coals or burner. We always use a cover when grilling over indirect heat.

direct grilling

two-zone grilling

indirect grilling

Secrets to Great Grilling

Here are the ten most important things to keep in mind when grilling:

1. **Know thy grill.** Your particular grill might be smaller or larger than the ones we used to test our dishes, or it could be a Big Green Egg. Adjust timing accordingly. Test for doneness when your food looks done.

2. **Marinate with a flat-bottomed vessel.** Use a baking dish, sheet pan, or even a plate to marinate. A flat bottom provides more surface area than a bowl, so the ingredients will better absorb the marinade.

3. **Make sure the coals are hot.** For charcoal grills, don't start grilling until the charcoal is fully lit, glowing, and covered in a fine gray ash. Use a hand fan to hasten this process.

4. **Preheat your grill.** Make sure the grill—and especially the cooking grate—is adequately preheated before starting to grill. Preheat the grate for at least 5 minutes. For a gas grill, close the cover to preheat.

5. **Brush and oil the cooking grate every time.** Repeat: brush and oil your cooking grate every time you grill to keep food from sticking to the grate. We can't emphasize this enough.

6. **Keep the vents open.** For charcoal grills, make sure the vents on the bottom and cover are open to allow oxygen to fuel your fire. Also, make sure the vents on the bottom aren't clogged, so air can get in.

7. **Use the cover strategically.** We'll tell you which foods must be grilled covered. The cover traps heat, so thick cuts of meat cook evenly, and also cuts the flow of oxygen, reducing flare-ups.

8. **Add more coals.** Keep the temperature consistent by adding more charcoal to the grill before the fire gets too weak. After coals burn for about 1 hour, it's time to replenish. For gas grills, always keep an extra tank on hand so you don't run out.

9. **Keep your grill clean.** Brush the cooking grate after grilling, while it's still hot. When the grill cools, scoop out the leftover ash. For gas grills, clean the briquettes or lava rocks once they cool and keep the gas jets unclogged. Wipe down the grill regularly with soap and water.

10. **Remember, grilling is an art.** That's the fun and beauty of it. When you're cooking over fire, you're really *cooking*—that's why we love grilling! So use your judgment: remember, the recipes in our book are guidelines. Grill according to your gut, your equipment, your ingredients, and your environment (grilling in Denver, the Mile High City, say, requires more time than grilling in Death Valley).

CLASSIC YAKITORI

SOUL FOOD, COMFORT FOOD, DRINKING FOOD— yakitori is all this and more. The word literally means "grilled bird," but yakitori can also include beef, pork, duck, and veggies. No matter which ingredients you use, yakitori is always bite-sized pieces, impaled on skewers, and grilled over fire, preferably one fueled with Japanese binchotan (see "Binchotan," page 12). Chicken remains the primary ingredient for yakitori—some old school joints serve nothing but—prepared either seasoned with salt or basted with *tare* (pronounced "tar-eh"), or sauce. But the *tare* isn't brushed on willy-nilly. The secret to great yakitori is grilling the chicken partway, coating with the sauce, and then grilling the coated chicken. So you grill both the chicken and the sauce. This one-two punch is the reason why yakitori comes out double-caramelized and so lip-smacking delicious. And it's why yakitori is one of the most popular and beloved foods in Japan.

Although there were references to it some two hundred years earlier, yakitori really caught the fancy of the general population in the nineteenth century when Japan reopened to the West and its citizens began consuming meat again (see "Meat in Japanese Cooking," page 2). Interestingly, the most prized meat at that time was chicken, not beef, and high-end "chicken cuisine" restaurants began popping up all over Japan, especially along routes to important shrines. It was the leftover bits of chicken from these restaurants that ended up spawning another enterprise: skewering and grilling scraps of chicken as yakitori. Eventually, yakitori became woven into the fabric of Japanese life, especially after World War II, with the skewers offered at *yatai* (mobile food stalls) and mom-and-pop joints. A singular yakitori culture and connoisseurship were born, with this simple cooking often raised to a level of culinary art. Customers enjoy every part of the chicken imaginable—and some unimaginable—and feast on heirloom breeds, birds of different ages, even fighting cock, reveling in a celebration of chicken-y flavors and textures. In fact, Tadashi's earliest childhood memories include tagging along as his father slipped out of the house to meet his pals for yakitori and beer at "Beautiful Land," the corner hole-in-the-wall where Tadashi developed a lifelong devotion to these skewers.

Because yakitori places are so widespread in Japan—and because most people there live in homes without outdoor space—grilling skewers is usually left to professional cooks. But here in America, where a Weber is almost a birthright, we've made it our mission to show you how you can prepare these delicious skewers at home. They're fast and easy to prepare; easy to handle on the grill; and, most importantly, easy to grab hold of and eat. Once you try yakitori at home, we personally guarantee you'll get hooked!

A couple of practical things to keep in mind:

- *Tare* or salt? Chicken yakitori is typically grilled two ways: double-caramelized with the *tare* or grilled straight up with just salt. Depending on the part of the bird, we suggest the most popular option in the recipes that follow, but feel free to switch if you'd prefer—ultimately it's up to you. Also, some chicken yakitori recipes, and some nonchicken yakitori, have other traditional flavor pairings, which we stick to, rather than the *tare* or salt.

• **Accents** We recommend the two primary accents, *shichimi togarashi* (page 7) and *sansho* (page 7), depending on the skewer; but again, feel free to switch up, or even mix the two together to make your own custom blend.

Setting Up Your Yakitori Grill: Foil Method and Brick Method

In Japan you can buy specialized yakitori *konro* (grills), rectangular-shaped, fireproofed ceramic boxes. These are long, narrow, and deep to make it easy to pile in *binchotan* (see "Binchotan," page 12) and concentrate the heat, suspend yakitori skewers over the glowing coals, and handle said skewers without roasting your hands. Instead of a fixed cooking grate, there's just a removable wire grid. And that's the beauty of it: without a grate, the yakitori can't stick to anything, so basting and turning are a snap. If you're a diehard yakitori *otaku* (fanatic), by all means order yourself one (see "Sources," page 177). For the rest of us, here are two foolproof ways to grill yakitori on any charcoal or gas grill.

THE FOIL METHOD   This is the simplest yakitori grilling method. Measure a sheet of aluminum foil the length of your grill and fold it in half. Carefully lay the folded sheet on one side of the grate. Now place the skewers on the grate so the exposed ends are resting on the aluminum foil, and the meat ends are over the fire. This way, the skewers, which are typically made from bamboo, won't burn. Be sure to brush and oil the grate beforehand, or the yakitori might stick when you turn the skewers. Also, since the yakitori is so close to the fire, be careful of flare-ups from dripping fat. Leave enough room on the grill to shift the skewers away from the flare-up and keep a water-filled spray bottle handy to douse pesky flames. Use tongs to handle the skewers, grasping the food, not the skewers.

THE BRICK METHOD   This method approximates a traditional Japanese *konro*. It's a little more involved than the foil method, but it gives you more control over grilling your skewers and is the method we use in our own backyards. For a standard-sized kettle grill ($22^1/_2$ inches in diameter) or gas grill, buy four bricks (8 by 4 by 2 inches each) and wrap with foil. Preheat your grill to medium-hot. Resting on the grate, arrange the bricks in two parallel rows directly over the fire; set the bricks on their long, narrow sides and about 4 inches apart. You want them just far enough apart to grill the yakitori but not burn the skewers. Use tongs or fireproof gloves to safely handle the bricks. Also, try lining up the bricks in such a way that your hands aren't over the fire when you turn the skewers (or use tongs to grasp the skewers and turn them). When you grill your yakitori, suspend the skewers between the bricks. *Very important:* Make sure your skewers have a full 4 inches of yakitori meat on them, so the bare skewers are not exposed between the bricks, just the meat; otherwise the skewers can burn. With the brick method, yakitori will cook perfectly and will be high enough from the heat that flare-ups can't reach them.

Skewers

Japanese grill cooks use a number of different *kushi* , or skewers, to grill foods. For yakitori grilling, these skewers are typically made from bamboo. The standard yakitori skewer is a *teppogushi*—or the "gun skewer" because of its shape. These skewers are flat with a tab on one end that makes them easy to turn. You can usually find them in Japanese markets. Flat skewers are another good choice for yakitori because they won't roll when placed on the grill. But if you can only find the ubiquitous 8-inch-long round bamboo skewers, they'll work, too; you just have to watch that they don't roll.

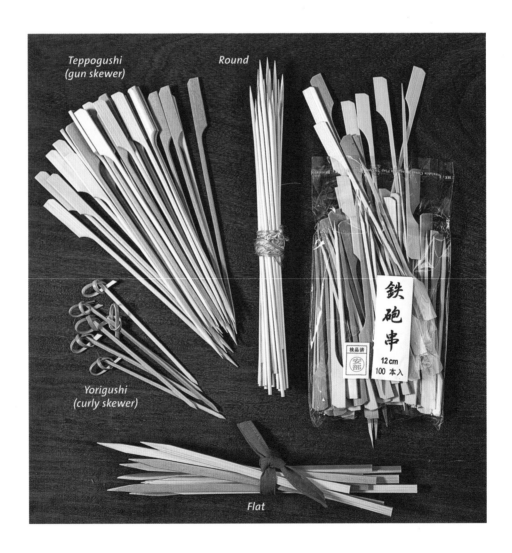

Classic Yakitori Sauce

Yakitori Tare

This is the basic version of the classic yakitori sauce Tadashi grew up with in Tokyo. Every yakitori joint in the city has its own secret recipe for this sauce; you can create your own version, too, by adding ginger, scallions, garlic, or black pepper (see Variation, following). Yakitori sauce can keep in the refrigerator for 1 month. After each use, boil the sauce for 2 minutes to kill any bacteria and evaporate any accumulated moisture. Let the sauce come to room temperature before returning it to the fridge. (It's fine if chicken fat accumulates on the surface; just mix together the next time you reheat.)

Makes 2 cups

Bones from 1 chicken (carcass and leg bones), coarsely chopped; bits of meat and skin are okay

2 cups mirin

2 cups soy sauce

1 cup sake

1 cup water

2 tablespoons packed brown sugar

Preheat an oven broiler. Arrange the chicken bones in a roasting pan. Place the pan under the heat. Broil until the bones are browned, about 5 minutes on each side, using tongs to turn the bones over.

Transfer the bones to a large stockpot. Add the mirin, soy sauce, sake, water, and brown sugar. Bring the stockpot to a boil over high heat. Decrease the heat to low and simmer, uncovered, until the liquid is reduced by half and becomes nice and glossy, at least 1 hour. Strain to remove the bones (and any optional ingredients) and discard. Let the liquid come to room temperature and use.

VARIATION Add one or more of the following to the stockpot with the other ingredients and follow the instructions above: 3 to 5 crushed cloves garlic; 1 bunch scallions (white and green parts or green part only); 1 to 2 ounces fresh ginger, thickly sliced; 1 to 2 teaspoons freshly ground black pepper.

Grilling Classic Yakitori

Grilling yakitori is not difficult, but you have to pay close attention to each skewer over the fire. Remember that yakitori is a two-part grilling technique: first you char the meat, then you caramelize the sauce you brush on the meat. To get your grill ready, see "Setting Up Your Takitori Grill: Foil Method and Brick Method," page 20.

Preheat a grill to medium-hot heat. Line your yakitori skewers in a row (the skewers can touch). The yakitori will take about 8 minutes to grill. Start by turning the skewers every 1 minute or so as they brown. Use tongs to turn the skewers; be careful not to burn the chicken. If you notice some skewers browning too fast over a hot spot, trade them with skewers grilling over a less hot part. And don't hesitate to shift skewers as you grill or spray flare-ups with water. When the meat becomes lightly browned and you can see it sizzling, after about 6 minutes, brush the sauce on top. Grill for about 2 minutes more, turning about every 30 seconds and brushing on more sauce each time. The chicken will become a rich auburn color and release an incredible roasted soy sauce aroma. Transfer the skewers to a platter, drip 1 tablespoon more sauce on top, and serve immediately. Accent with *shichimi togarashi*.

Old-School Tare

If you amble into an old-school yakitori joint in Japan and pay close attention to the grilling, you'll notice two things: First, you'll never see the cooks brushing sauce on the yakitori; instead, they dunk skewers in an earthenware jar filled with the *tare* to coat them. And if you hang around until closing time, you'll also realize the *tare* is never boiled at the end of the day (as we might do here to kill bacteria), even after countless skewers of semicooked chicken have been dipped into it. What's going on? *Mannen tare*—"10,000 year" sauce—that's what. As skewers are dipped into the sauce, the fat and protein of the chicken combine with the flavor compounds of the soy sauce and emulsify, which the sugar stabilizes. Practically, this means that every dip of a skewer creates more complexity inside that jar, and the *tare* begins to act like living sourdough starter. Cooks keep alive the bacteria and yeasts developing inside by adding more *tare* ingredients over time, the *tare* jars become distinctive environments, ones that give the skewers of different yakitori joints their own singular taste. We don't advise you to create your own *mannen tare*—leave that to the pros.

How to Skewer Yakitori

1. Always skewer ingredients on a flat work surface.

2. Thread the skewers into ingredients with a twisting motion.

3. Press down on the skewers with heel of your hand to compress ingredients.

4. Lightly salt ingredients on both sides, even if using *tare* (yakitori sauce).

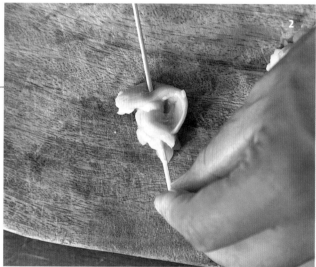

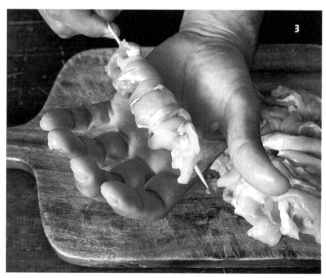

Classic Chicken Leg

Momo

This is the most basic yakitori. Basic, but fantastic. When Tadashi was a kid, he'd grab a couple of *momo* from the yakitori shack on the corner almost every day on his way home from school. Once he smelled that charring chicken wafting from the grill, it was game over (and at less than the equivalent of fifty cents a skewer, at the time, even a kid could indulge). Chicken legs have it all: flavorful, juicy, tender, chewy, rich meat that pairs perfectly with savory-sweet *tare*. Some folks prefer no *tare*, just salt, which is fine, too—for a purer chicken flavor. Grill the same length of time, but omit the marinade.

Makes about
12 skewers

4 boneless, skinless whole chicken legs (legs and thighs), about 1 1/2 pounds

Salt

1/2 cup Classic Yakitori Sauce (Yakitori Tare, page 23)

Shichimi togarashi (page 7), for accent

Cut the chicken with the grain into 1/2-inch-wide slices. Prepare the skewers by folding each slice in half and skewering, making sure that the folded sides are aligned, for aesthetic reasons. As you work, turn the skewer in a screwing motion to make it easier to pierce the meat. Each skewer will hold about 5 chicken slices, covering about 4 inches of length of skewer. When the skewers are ready, gently press down on each one with the heel of your hand to compact the meat (see "How to Skewer Yakitori," page 25). Lightly season all sides with salt. Follow "Grilling Classic Yakitori," page 24. Serve immediately.

Chicken and Scallion

Negima

Adding scallions to *momo* (Classic Chicken Leg) creates this popular yakitori variation. The onion adds crunch and a bit of sharpness that stands up to the rich chicken. In Japan, you'd skewer the white part of *negi*, a Japanese variety of long onion with a sharp taste that turns sweet and tender when cooked, rather than scallion. If you can find *negi*, use it; otherwise, scallions do the trick. This yakitori also tastes great simply salted, without *tare*.

Makes about
15 skewers

4 boneless, skinless whole chicken legs (legs and thighs), about 1¹/₂ pounds

15 scallions (white part only), cut into 1-inch-long pieces

Salt

¹/₂ cup Classic Yakitori Sauce (Yakitori Tare, page 23)

Shichimi togarashi (page 7), for accent

Cut the chicken with the grain into ¹/₂-inch-wide slices. Prepare the skewers by folding each slice in half and skewering, alternating each chicken slice with a piece of scallion lined up perpendicular to the skewer and pierced through the center. Make sure that the folded sides of the chicken are aligned, for aesthetic reasons. As you work, turn the skewer in a screwing motion to make it easier to pierce the meat and scallion. Each skewer will hold about 4 chicken slices and 3 scallion pieces, covering about 4 inches of length of skewer. When the skewers are ready, gently press down on each one with the heel of your hand to compact the meat (see "How to Skewer Yakitori," page 25). Lightly season all sides with salt. Follow "Grilling Classic Yakitori," page 24.

Minced Chicken

Tsukune

A yakitori chef from the chicken-loving city Nagoya shared the secret to amazing *tsukune* with Tadashi: precook some of the ground chicken, cool it, and mix it in with the raw ground chicken to give the *tsukune* an irresistible fluffy, springy texture. Here's another secret to this yakitori, this time from us: Don't pack on too much chicken when you're forming the skewers; use a scoop about the size of a golf ball for each skewer. Also, since there's no binder in the mixture (no eggs or breadcrumbs, for example), knead the chicken mixture until it becomes sticky and clings together. Use flat skewers, if possible (see "Skewers," page 22); the ground chicken adheres to them better.

Makes about 16 skewers

1 pound ground chicken (preferably all dark meat), divided into 1/3- and 2/3-pound portions

1 tablespoon red miso (page 6)

1/2 cup finely chopped scallions (green and white parts)

1 tablespoon sesame oil, plus more to coat your hands

1 bunch shiso leaves (about 10 leaves), very thinly sliced (optional)

Salt

1/2 cup Classic Yakitori Sauce (Yakitori Tare, page 23)

Shichimi togarashi (page 7), for accent

Preheat a dry skillet over medium heat. When the skillet is hot, add 1/3 pound ground chicken. Cook and stir until the chicken turns white, about 5 minutes. Make sure not to brown the chicken you just want to it cook through. As it cooks, use a fork to break up the ground chicken into the smallest pieces possible. Transfer the cooked chicken to a plate and let it come to room temperature.

When the chicken has cooled, mix it with the 2/3 pound chicken, miso, scallions, 1 tablespoon sesame oil, and shiso in a large bowl. Knead the mixture until it becomes sticky and binds together. Lightly coat your hands with sesame oil so the chicken mixture won't stick to them. Scoop a handful of the chicken mixture and form it into an oval patty by flipping it in the palm of one hand and gently squeezing until it compacts and elongates to about 4 inches in length. Now press a skewer lengthwise onto the patty and form the mixture around it; it should look like a mini corn dog. Place the skewer on a tray and gently flatten it with your fist. Repeat with the remaining mixture. When you're done, lightly season all sides with salt. Follow "Grilling Classic Yakitori," page 24. Serve immediately.

Chicken Liver

Kimo

In Japan, the most popular ways to enjoy chicken liver are stir-fried with garlic chives; braised with soy sauce, sugar, sake and ginger; and this way—as delicious yakitori. The pronounced flavor of the liver pairs nicely with the yakitori *tare*, so brush it on liberally.

Makes about 12 skewers

1 pound chicken livers

Salt

½ cup Classic Yakitori Sauce (Yakitori Tare, page 23)

Shichimi togarashi (page 7), for accent

Add the chicken livers to a bowl filled with cold water and soak them for 10 minutes to wash. Rinse the livers under cold, running water and drain in a colander. Cut each liver into 4 pieces, trimming away any excess fat or congealed blood you may find inside the liver. Skewer the liver (about 4 pieces per skewer), so the liver covers about 4 inches of length of skewer. As you work, turn the skewer in a screwing motion to make it easier to pierce the meat (see "How to Skewer Yakitori," page 25). Follow "Grilling Classic Yakitori," page 24.

Chicken: Before and After

Who knew that one chicken could produce so many different yakitori? We found some thirty distinct chicken parts skewered as yakitori. Some of these are a bit esoteric, like the inner thigh, outer thigh, base of the heart, coxcomb, and windpipe. Others have evocative names, like "fist" (knee cartilage), "Japanese emperor oak" (thigh), "drawstring purse" (male reproductive organs), and "long-sleeve kimono" (shoulder meat). Here are the most popular:

Thigh	Tenderloin	Liver	Neck
Wing	Oyster	Heart	Tail
Breast	Gizzard	Skin	*Tsukune*

Gizzard

Sunagimo

Gizzards are prized in Japan more for their springy, crunchy texture than for their dense flavor, which falls somewhere between leg meat and liver. But gizzards can get tough as they grill. So if you steam them as they grill by spraying them with water a few times, they'll stay tender. Keep a misting bottle handy; alternatively, you can flick a little water on them with your fingertips.

Makes about
12 skewers

¾ **pound chicken gizzards, trimmed of excess fat**

Salt

Shichimi togarashi (page 7), for accent

Cut each gizzard in half. Skewer the gizzard pieces (about 5 per skewer) so the pieces cover about 4 inches of skewer. As you work, turn the skewer in a screwing motion to make it easier to pierce the gizzards (see "How to Skewer Yakitori," page 25). Lightly season all sides with salt.

Choose your yakitori grilling method (see "Setting Up Your Yakitori Grill: Foil Method and Brick Method," page 20), then preheat a grill to medium-hot. Grill 4 to 5 minutes, turning the skewers every minute or so as they brown. Don't hesitate to shift skewers as you grill, especially if you notice some skewers browning too fast over a hot spot; trade them with skewers grilling over a less hot part. Lightly mist the gizzards with water 2 to 3 times while grilling. When they're ready, the gizzards will shrink, and their surface will look dry. Serve immediately. Accent with *shichimi togarashi*.

Neck

Seseri

Consider neck a "cult" yakitori. In Japan, the incredibly tender and flavorful neck meat is often laboriously pulled off the bone, then grilled; it's a prized delicacy, not easy to find. We love neck, too, but prefer to skewer and grill it whole, another popular option, which is easier, and we think even tastier, because the bones impart their flavor and juices while grilling. Eat the neck like corn on the cob, discarding the bones.

Makes about
10 skewers

**1 pound chicken necks
(about 10 necks), skinned**

Salt

Push skewers through the hollow spinal column of the necks (the hole in the center of the neck, so the skewer will thread right through the neck bones). Lightly season all sides with salt.

Choose your yakitori grilling method (see "Setting Up Your Yakitori Grill: Foil Method and Brick Method," page 20); preheat a grill to medium-hot. Grill for about 8 minutes, turning the skewers every 2 minutes so all 4 sides brown. Don't hesitate to shift skewers as you grill, especially if you notice some skewers browning too fast over a hot spot; trade them with skewers grilling over a less hot part. Serve immediately.

Chicken Heart

Hatsu

Heart is another yakitori delicacy—there's only one per chicken, after all. Juicy and tender, heart goes great with a frosty mug of Japanese beer.

Makes about 12 skewers

³/₄ pound chicken hearts, trimmed of fat and halved

Salt

Shichimi togarashi (page 7), for accent

Wash the heart pieces under cold, running water to remove any blood; pat dry. Skewer the heart pieces (about 5 halves per skewer) so the pieces cover about 4 inches of skewer. As you work, turn the skewer in a screwing motion to make it easier to pierce the hearts (see "How to Skewer Yakitori," page 25). Lightly season all sides with salt.

Choose your yakitori grilling method (see "Setting Up Your Yakitori Grill: Foil Method and Brick Method," page 20); preheat a grill to medium-hot. Grill for about 2 minutes, turning the skewers once. Serve immediately. Accent with *shichimi togarashi*.

Skin

Kawa

Grilling the skin—an iconic yakitori dish—is the true test of any yakitori master. In fact, this seemingly simple, two-ingredient recipe is the most difficult one in the book. Why? The goal here is to get the skin crunchy and crispy on the outside, but keep it juicy and tender on the inside. But there's a problem: that blubbery layer of yellow fat under the skin, which drips, drips, drips nonstop as you grill, triggering one spectacular flare-up after the other. What to do? Shift and turn, shift and turn, and use a spray bottle early and often to douse the flames. Keep those skewers moving one step ahead of the flare-ups, and you'll earn your stripes as a yakitori cook.

Makes about
12 skewers

Skin of 1 whole chicken, cut into ¹/₂-inch-wide strips

Salt

Skewer the skin strips by folding the skin over itself in layers, so the skin covers about 4 inches of length of skewer. Lightly season all sides with salt.

Choose your yakitori grilling method (see "Setting Up Your Yakitori Grill: Foil Method and Brick Method," page 20); preheat a grill to medium. Grill about 6 minutes, turning the skewers every 20 seconds or so as they brown. Don't let the skin burn; you want the skin to become crispy. Don't hesitate to shift skewers as you grill or spray flare-ups with water, especially if you notice some skewers browning too fast over a hot spot; trade them with skewers grilling over a less hot part.

Serve immediately.

Chicken Oysters

Solares

Oysters are the two little jewels of meat nestled on either side of the backbone by the thigh. They might just be the most flavorful bit of chicken on the bird, so simply salt them and grill. But there's a rub—they're also the most difficult part of the chicken to find. If you can get your hands on oysters, great; otherwise, keep them in mind if you ever find yourself at an old-school yakitori joint in Japan.

Makes about
12 skewers

1 pound chicken oysters

Salt

Sansho (page 7), for accent

Skewer the chicken oysters by piercing them lengthwise (about 4 oysters per skewer) so they cover about 4 inches of length of skewer. As you work, turn the skewers in a screwing motion to make it easier to pierce the oysters (see "How to Skewer Yakitori," page 25). Lightly season all sides with salt.

Choose your yakitori grilling method (see "Setting Up Your Yakitori Grill: Foil Method and Brick Method," page 20); preheat a grill to medium-hot. Grill for about 6 minutes, turning the skewers about every 2 minutes, until the oysters are browned. Serve immediately. Accent with *sansho*.

How Much Yakitori for Dinner?

Japanese typically eat yakitori as either a tasty side dish or the main event. In a supporting role, three skewers per person is plenty, but if you're planning an all-yakitori-all-the-time kind of meal, a.k.a. "Yakitori Night" (a night we can't recommend enough), plan on at least six skewers per person. Make sure to mix the types of skewers, using different cuts of chicken, plus veggies, pork, or even beef tongue—you'll find recipes for all of these yakitori in this chapter. The point is to experience different foods, textures, and flavors and, most importantly, have fun doing it—that's what yakitori eating is all about.

Chicken Breast with Wasabi

Shiromi Wasabi Yaki

Tender breast meat and wasabi are a classic combination, wasabi's subtle heat pairs wonderfully with the juicy breast and brings out its flavor. We add oil to the wasabi so this lean piece of chicken doesn't dry out while grilling.

Makes about 12 skewers

¼ cup wasabi

1 tablespoon plus 1 teaspoon vegetable oil

3 boneless, skinless chicken breasts (about 1 pound), cut into 1-inch cubes

Salt

Mix the wasabi and vegetable oil in a bowl to make the marinade; set aside.

Skewer the cubes of chicken (about 3 pieces per portion) so the chicken covers about 4 inches of skewer. Lightly season all sides with salt.

Choose your yakitori grilling method (see "Setting Up Your Yakitori Grill: Foil Method and Brick Method," page 20); preheat a grill to medium-hot. Grill for about 3 minutes, turning once. Brush a thick layer of wasabi marinade on top of the chicken. Grill for about 2 minutes more, turning once, and brushing on more marinade. The chicken meat will turn white when ready. Serve immediately.

Chicken Tenderloins with Ume Paste

Sasami

The Japanese name *sasami* means "bamboo leaf," a poetic evocation that brings to mind this long, thin strip of chicken, pulled off the inside of the breast. The *ume* paste gives the tenderloins a tangy, salty accent.

Makes about
12 skewers

3 tablespoons ume paste (page 7)

1 tablespoon plus 1 teaspoon sake

1 tablespoon plus 1 teaspoon vegetable oil

12 chicken tenderloins (about 1 pound)

Salt

1 bunch shiso leaves (about 10 leaves), finely chopped, for garnish

Mix together the *ume* paste, sake, and vegetable oil in a bowl to make the marinade; set aside.

Skewer the tenderloins lengthwise (1 tenderloin per skewer) so the meat covers at least 4 inches of length of skewer. Lightly season all sides with salt.

Choose your yakitori grilling method (see "Setting Up Your Yakitori Grill: Foil Method and Brick Method," page 20); pre-heat a grill to medium-hot. Grill for about 3 minutes, turning once. Brush the *ume* marinade on top of the chicken. Grill for about 2 minutes more, turning once, and brushing on more marinade. Sprinkle the shiso on top and serve immediately.

Ume-Wasabi Duck Breast

Kamo Ume Wasabi

The *ume* paste and wasabi here cut the fattiness and gaminess of the duck. Be careful of flare-ups as duck fat drips onto the coals.

Makes about
12 skewers

**3 tablespoons ume paste
(page 7)**

2 tablespoons wasabi

**1 tablespoon plus
1 teaspoon mirin**

**2 duck breasts
(about 1¹/₂ pounds)**

**12 scallions (white parts
only), cut into 1¹/₂-inch
pieces**

Mix together the *ume* paste, wasabi, and mirin in a bowl to make the marinade; set aside.

Trim the extra fat from the duck breasts and halve them lengthwise. Cut each half into ¹/₂-inch-thick slices. Lay the slices flat on a work surface and skewer through the center, alternating duck breast and scallion (about 3 pieces of duck and 2 pieces of scallion per skewer) so the ingredients cover about 4 inches of skewer. As you work, turn the skewer in a screwing motion to make it easier to pierce the meat (see "How to Skewer Yakitori," page 25).

Choose your yakitori grilling method (see "Setting Up Your Yakitori Grill: Foil Method and Brick Method," page 20); preheat a grill to medium-hot. Grill for about 3 minutes, turning once. Brush a thick layer of *ume*-wasabi marinade on top of the duck. Grill for about 1 minute more, turning once and brushing on more marinade. Don't hesitate to spray flare-ups with water or shift skewers as you grill, especially if you notice some skewers browning too fast over a hot spot; trade them with skewers grilling over a less hot part. The duck will be sizzling and crispy when ready. Serve immediately.

Bacon Asparagus

Aspara Bacon

Every *izakaya* (eating pub) in Japan offers this iconic yakitori on its menu. Bacon and asparagus are a perfect combination, the salty, fatty pork adding incredible flavor to the spears. As the bacon crisps up, the asparagus cooks through but still remains crunchy, the texture you're shooting for.

Makes about
12 skewers

1 pound bacon, thinly sliced and cut into 3-inch strips

1 pound asparagus (preferably jumbo), trimmed and cut into 1½-inch pieces

1 lemon, quartered

Wrap a strip of bacon around each piece of asparagus. Skewer these rolled pieces (about 4 per skewer) so they cover about 4 inches of skewer.

Choose your yakitori grilling method (see "Setting Up Your Yakitori Grill: Foil Method and Brick Method," page 20); preheat a grill to medium-hot. Grill for about 6 minutes, turning the skewers about every 2 minutes as they brown. Don't hesitate to shift skewers as you grill, especially if you notice some skewers browning too fast over a hot spot; trade them with skewers grilling over a less hot part. The bacon will crisp up and sizzle when the skewers are ready. Squeeze lemon juice on the skewers and serve immediately.

Pork Belly

Ton Negima

In some parts of Japan, *yakiton* (skewered, grilled pork) is even more popular than grilled chicken. The area of Tokyo where Tadashi grew up was chock full of these spots. *Yakiton* joints grill every part of the pig, and we mean every part—cheek, jowl, brain, guts, some twenty different parts. In fact, Tadashi's favorites back in the day included *kashira* (head) and *nodo* (throat), which is both crunchy and meaty. Assuming your local supermarket doesn't carry *nodo*, we thought to share another kind of *yakiton*, the iconic and hugely popular *ton negima*, pork belly and scallion.

Makes about
12 skewers

1 pound fresh pork belly, cut into ¹/₄-inch-thick slices (about 1¹/₂ inches wide)

2 bunches scallions (white part only), cut into 1¹/₂-inch pieces

Salt

Sansho (page 7), for accent

Thread the skewers by alternating the pork belly and scallion (about 3 pieces of pork belly and 2 pieces of scallion per skewer) so the pieces cover about 4 inches of skewer. As you work, turn the skewers in a screwing motion to make it easier to pierce the pork and scallion (see "How to Skewer Yakitori," page 25). When the skewers are ready, gently press down on each one with the heel of your hand to compact the meat. Lightly season all sides with salt.

Choose your yakitori grilling method (see "Setting Up Your Yakitori Grill: Foil Method and Brick Method," page 20); preheat a grill to medium-hot. Grill for 5 to 6 minutes, turning the skewers every minute to brown. Be careful not to burn the pork belly. Don't hesitate to spray flare-ups with water or shift skewers as you grill, especially if you notice some skewers browning too fast over a hot spot, you trade them with skewers grilling over a less hot part. Serve immediately. Accent with *sansho*.

Beef Liver

Gyu Reba

Beef liver has a more steak-like texture than chicken liver. It's enjoyed raw in Japan and also skewered and grilled as yakitori. You can also use calf's liver, which is more tender and delicate.

Makes about 12 skewers

1 pound beef liver, ¹/₂ inch thick

Salt

1 lemon, quartered

Trim the membrane and excess fat from the liver and cut out any veins. Cut the liver into approximately 1-inch squares. Skewer the liver (about 4 pieces per skewer) so the pieces cover about 4 inches of skewer. As you work, turn the skewers in a screwing motion to make it easier to pierce the liver (see "How to Skewer Yakitori," page 25). Lightly season all sides with salt.

Choose your yakitori grilling method (see "Setting Up Your Yakitori Grill: Foil Method and Brick Method," page 20); preheat a grill to medium-hot. Grill for about 4 minutes, turning the skewers once. Squeeze lemon juice on the liver and serve immediately.

Beef Tongue

Gyutan

Connoisseurs of beef-tongue *yakitori* prize the various parts of the tongue for different flavor and texture sensations. The tip is chewier and denser, while the back of the tongue is richer and beefier. If you're *gyutan otaku* (tongue-meat obsessed), make sure to skewer each part separately, and compare and contrast.

Makes about
12 skewers

1 beef tongue (about 2 pounds)

Salt

Sansho (page 7), for accent

1 lemon, quartered

Prepare an ice bath and set aside. Add the tongue to a large pot, cover with water, and bring to a boil over high heat. Boil for 2 minutes; transfer the tongue to the ice bath. As soon as it cools, peel off the skin and slice the tongue into 1/4-inch-thick slices. Prepare the skewers by folding each slice in half and skewering through the center, making sure that the folded sides are aligned. As you work, turn the skewer in a screwing motion to make it easier to pierce the meat (see "How to Skewer Yakitori," page 25). Each skewer will hold about 5 pieces of tongue, covering about 4 inches of skewer. Lightly season all sides with salt.

Choose your yakitori grilling method (see "Setting Up Your Yakitori Grill: Foil Method and Brick Method," page 20); preheat a grill to medium-hot. Grill for 3 to 4 minutes, turning the skewers every 1 minute or so to brown. Serve immediately. Accent with *sansho* and a squeeze of lemon juice.

Shiitake Mushrooms

Shiitake

While chicken is considered the classic yakitori, veggies grilled on skewers are also enormously popular in Japan, for good reason: Grilled vegetables are easy to prepare, fast to cook, and taste delicious. Case in point, shiitake, which firms up as it grills, and its incredible flavor becomes more concentrated.

Makes 12 skewers

24 shiitake mushrooms (about ³/₄ pound), stemmed

¹/₂ cup fresh lime or lemon juice

2 tablespoons soy sauce

2 tablespoons olive oil

Cut the mushrooms in half on an angle. Use the double-skewer method (see "Double-Skewering Vegetables," page 45) to truss the mushrooms (4 pieces per double-skewer) to cover about 4 inches of skewer. For aesthetic reasons, make sure all the shiitake pieces are lined up in the same direction (for example, the sliced side toward the back). Set aside.

Mix together the lime juice, soy sauce, and olive oil in a bowl to make the marinade. Pour the marinade onto a baking dish or rimmed sheet pan. Lay the skewers in the marinade and flip them 4 times to generously coat each side of the mushrooms.

Choose your yakitori grilling method (see "Setting Up Your Yakitori Grill: Foil Method and Brick Method," page 20); preheat a grill to medium-hot. Grill for about 2 minutes, turning once, until the shiitake become juicy and lightly browned. Be careful not to burn the mushrooms. Serve immediately.

VARIATION Try this method with *shimeji, maitake,* oyster, or crimini mushrooms.

Shishito Peppers

Shishito

Shishito peppers are bright green Japanese peppers about three inches long and extremely popular in Japan (you can usually find them in Japanese markets here). The *shishito* shrink and blister as they grill and release an incredibly peppery aroma. These peppers are mostly mild—mostly, because every once in a while you'll bite into a spicy one! You can grill the *shishito* with salt instead of soy sauce, too, also irresistible. Just lightly season all sides with salt and follow the instructions below.

Makes about
10 skewers

½ cup soy sauce

2 tablespoons sake

40 shishito peppers (about ¾ pound)

Whisk together the soy sauce and sake in a bowl to make the marinade; set aside.

Use the double skewer method to truss the *shishito* peppers (4 pieces per double skewer) to cover about 4 inches of skewer. Set aside.

Choose your yakitori grilling method (see "Setting Up Your Yakitori Grill: Foil Method and Brick Method," page 20); preheat a grill to medium. Grill the peppers for about 1 minute, then turn and brush with the marinade. Grill for about 2 minutes more, turning every 30 seconds. Brush on more marinade after each turn. The *shishito* peppers will shrink and blister when they're done. Serve immediately.

Asparagus

Aspara

Simply salt the asparagus and grill it until it chars a little. Don't overcook; you want crispy, crunchy asparagus, not a mushy spear.

Makes about
12 skewers

12 jumbo asparagus

Salt

Trim and peel the stem ends of the asparagus and cut each one into 4 pieces. Use the double-skewer method (see "Double-Skewering Vegetables," page 45) to truss the asparagus (4 pieces per double skewer) to cover about 4 inches of skewer. Lightly season all sides with salt.

Choose your yakitori grilling method (see "Setting Up Your Yakitori Grill: Foil Method and Brick Method," page 20); preheat a grill to medium. Grill for about 2 minutes, turning once, until the asparagus turns bright green and juicy. Serve immediately.

VARIATION Use this method to salt-grill scallions or *negi*, white parts only, cut into 1¹/₂-inch pieces.

Garlic

Nin-niku

Grilling transforms the garlic, mellowing its sharpness and turning it sublimely sweet, with a texture like a cooked potato. Peel the garlic under warm running water, which makes the skin soggy and easier to come off.

Makes 10 skewers

50 large whole cloves garlic, peeled

Salt

Skewer the garlic cloves with a single skewer (about 5 per skewer) so that they cover about 4 inches of skewer. Liberally season all sides with salt.

Choose your yakitori grilling method (see "Setting Up Your Yakitori Grill: Foil Method and Brick Method," page 20); preheat a grill to medium. Grill for about 2 minutes, turning once, until the garlic browns. Serve immediately.

Double-Skewering Vegetables

Use two parallel skewers to truss vegetables and keep the ingredients in place, that way they grill evenly and don't fall through the grate.

1. Skewer ingredients on a flat work surface.

2. Thread skewers into ingredients with a twisting motion.

3. After the first skewer is in place, hold the ingredients in place with the flat of your hand and twist in the second skewer.

4. Grill using the foil method or the brick method (see "Setting Up Your Yakitori Grill: Foil Method and Brick Method," page 20).

POULTRY

WHEN THE JAPANESE EMPEROR banned eating chicken in 676 A.D., it wasn't because he had an aversion to drumsticks. Back then, roosters were the time keepers, their cock-a-doodle-doos heralding the start of the day—and the emperor didn't want his subjects to cook their clocks. Chickens also were considered sacred and kept as pets, while cocks, besides their timely crowing, were bred for fighting. Eventually, Japan instituted a Buddhist edict prohibiting the killing and eating of all animals, more or less, although wild game and fowl such as pheasant, sparrow, and duck continued to be hunted despite the ban. Edict or not, by the seventeenth century chicken recipes started appearing in cookbooks, and when Westerners arrived in the mid-nineteenth, they brought along their meat-eating ways. Chicken became a popular food at that time, with the introduction of upscale "chicken cuisine" restaurants and the grilling of chicken on skewers—yakitori—catching fire, so to speak, with the public. Not only did eating chicken get a reprieve, but breeding them did, too: farmers started raising *jidori*, Japanese free-range heirloom chickens with at least 50 percent of the bird's lineage coming from indigenous stock. Today, there are some fifty recognized *jidori* breeds in Japan, all of them celebrated, with some achieving cult status. The city of Nagoya is proud of its *Cochin* variety, which is eaten grilled, cooked, and raw. Further south, Kagoshima's *Stasuma* variety is also eaten raw, among other ways (also called *asadori*—morning chicken—because these free-range birds are slaughtered the morning they're going to be eaten). And in far northern snow country, Akita's famed *Hinai-jidori* are raised to the strains of Mozart to soothe them before they're butchered.

In the recipes that follow, we introduce traditional Japanese favorites, including the original teriyaki, as well as techniques that reflect how we grill here in America, like preparing half chickens. All of our dishes, though, reflect the Japanese sensibility of not doing too much to the bird and using seasonings to highlight the natural, delicious taste of the ingredient, but never overwhelm it. Finally, we urge you to grill with the freshest, highest quality fowl you can find.

HOW TO CUT A WHOLE CHICKEN

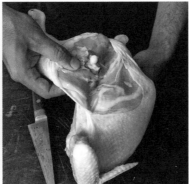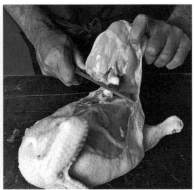

1.   Cut and remove legs

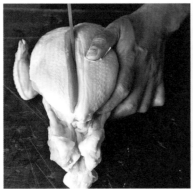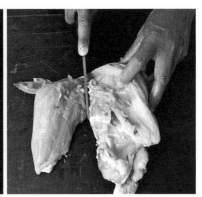

2.   Cut and separate breasts

3.   Portioned chicken

HOW TO BONE A CHICKEN LEG

1. Start at inside of leg at drumstick
2. Follow bone with knife
3. Cut along bone on the other side
4. Cut joint (but don't cut meat)
5. Flip chicken and fold over; cut around joint
6. Hold thigh bone with knife; pull off meat
7. Separate the leg bone
8. Pull leg bone out and cut it off
9. Boned chicken leg

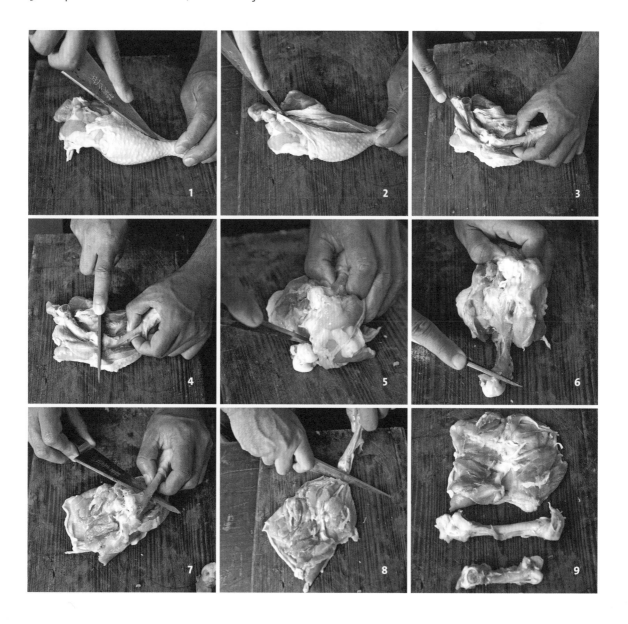

Grilled Chicken Breast Teriyaki

After sushi, chicken teriyaki is probably the most popular Japanese dish in America. But the teriyaki sauce we usually see here, typically a gummy gravy drenching chicken, is not the same as in Japan. The authentic version is a light, thin glaze that adds flavor and coats the chicken with an appealing sheen—in fact, teriyaki literally means "glossy grilled." The mirin and sugar create that luster, and the more you brush on the marinade while grilling, the glossier your chicken will become. Teriyaki is simple to prepare and also works great with swordfish (page 79).

Serves 4

¼ cup plus 2 tablespoons soy sauce

2 tablespoons sake

¼ cup mirin

1 tablespoon sugar

4 boneless, skinless chicken breast halves (about 2 pounds)

Shichimi togarashi (page 7), for accent

To make the teriyaki sauce, combine the ¼ cup soy sauce, sake, mirin, and sugar in a saucepan and bring to a boil over high heat. Boil for 30 seconds. Remove from heat and set aside.

Pour the remaining 2 tablespoons soy sauce in a shallow bowl. Dip the chicken breasts in the soy sauce to flavor them.

Preheat a grill to medium. Grill the chicken until browned and glossy, about 10 minutes, flipping every 2 minutes, and brushing on the teriyaki sauce after each turn. Let the chicken rest for 2 minutes, accent with the *shichimi togarashi*, and serve.

Chicken Breasts with Yuzu Kosho Marinade

Teriyaki isn't the only way to make magic with ho-hum chicken breasts. Here's another. The *yuzu kosho* marinade in this recipe adds flavor, fat, and a nice kick; the upshot, delicious chicken, every time.

Serves 4

4 boneless, skinless chicken breast halves (about 2 pounds)

¾ cup Yuzu Kosho Marinade (page 74)

Preheat a grill to medium heat. Grill the chicken until browned and glossy, about 10 minutes, flipping every 2 minutes, and brushing on the marinade after each turn. Let the chicken rest for 2 minutes. Slice and serve.

Bone-In Chicken Breast with Soy Sauce

One of Tadashi's culinary mantras is, "I love to cook birds with bones." Why bones? The chicken's skeleton acts as a conduit for heat, so it helps cook the inside of the bird while you grill it. And as it cooks, the bones release their own juices and flavors, so the meat turns out incredibly tasty and moist. Case in point, this dish. You'll be amazed how tender this breast turns out, and so appealing, too, lavished with soy sauce and other traditional Japanese flavors.

Serves 4

1 tablespoon rice vinegar

1 tablespoon mirin

1 tablespoon sake

2 teaspoons shichimi togarashi (page 7)

2 teaspoons sansho (page 7)

1 tablespoon grated fresh ginger

1 tablespoon sesame oil

1/2 cup soy sauce

4 bone-in chicken breast halves (3 to 4 pounds)

Mix together the rice vinegar, mirin, sake, *shichimi togarashi*, *sansho*, ginger, sesame oil, and soy sauce in a bowl to make the marinade. Pour three-fourths of the marinade into a baking dish or rimmed sheet pan; reserve the rest for brushing on the chicken as it grills. Lay the chicken breasts in the marinade and flip them 4 times to generously coat all sides. Once they're coated, marinate the chicken for 15 minutes.

Preheat a grill to medium heat. Remove the chicken from the marinade. Grill the chicken, covered, for a total of about 20 minutes this way: Start by grilling the chicken skin side down for about 9 minutes. Flip the chicken, brush on the reserved marinade, and grill for another 9 minutes. Grill the chicken for 2 minutes more, flipping twice, and brushing on more marinade after each turn. The breasts are ready when they are browned and glossy. Test for doneness using "The 'Nick-and-Peek' Method" (page 111). Let the chicken rest for 3 minutes. Slice and serve.

Pounded Chicken Breasts with Yukari Shiso Marinade

Here's a quick and tasty method to grill chicken breasts. Because they're pounded into thin cutlets, they grill fast and won't dry out. We use *yukari* shiso salt, made from the dried leaves of purple shiso, to add a tangy kick. If you have trouble finding this ingredient, substitute another flavored Japanese salt like *matcha* salt (powdered green tea salt). Once you marinate, use aluminum foil sheets to conveniently transfer the cutlets to the grill, but remove before grilling.

Serves 4

4 boneless, skinless chicken breast halves (about 2 pounds)

3 tablespoons yukari shiso salt

½ cup olive oil

3 tablespoons sake

1 tablespoon soy sauce

1 bunch shiso (about 10 leaves), coarsely chopped, for garnish

Butterfly the chicken breasts by cutting them almost all the way through along one long side; open like a book (or ask your butcher to butterfly the breasts). Wrap each piece of chicken in plastic wrap. Using a meat pounder, mallet, or the side of a heavy knife or cleaver, pound the chicken breasts until flattened to about ¼ inch thick. Make sure to pound both sides of the meat.

Mix together the *yukari* shiso salt, olive oil, sake, and soy sauce in a bowl to make the marinade. Pour three-fourths of the marinade into a baking dish or rimmed sheet pan; reserve the rest. Lay the breasts in the marinade and flip them 4 times to generously coat all over. Place each marinated breast on its own sheet of aluminum foil. You can stack the breasts on the foil, one on top of the other, for easy transport to the grill. (Remove the aluminum foil before grilling.)

Preheat the grill to high. Grill for about 1 minute, then flip and brush on the reserved marinade. Grill for 1 to 2 minutes more, flipping again, and brushing on more marinade. The breasts grill quickly; as soon as they're browned, they're done. Be careful not to overcook. Sprinkle with the chopped shiso and serve.

Sansho-Rubbed Butterflied Chicken Legs

Here's a trick culled from Japanese *makanai* (restaurant staff meal) cooking. Instead of boning the chicken legs, which takes precious time cooks don't have to spend on their own dinners, butterfly them by exposing the bone. This way, the bone helps transmit heat during grilling, so the chicken cooks more quickly and more evenly, and infuses the leg meat with its own incredible flavor and juices. The *sancho* adds wonderful fragrance, too.

Serves 4

4 whole chicken legs (legs and thighs), about 2 pounds

Sansho (page 7)

Salt

For each leg, cut open the leg to expose the leg bone and butterfly the meat: Insert a utility knife at the tip of the drumstick and slice along the bone, following the bone on the inside of the leg, along the crook, all the way to the end of the thigh. Use your hands to spread the meat away from the other side of the bone. Be very careful while cutting, making sure to keep your fingers out of the way. Once butterflied, liberally season the legs with *sansho* and salt all over.

Preheat a grill for a two-zone fire (hot and medium heat; see page 14). Grill the legs, starting with the skin side down, on hot heat for about 4 minutes, turning once. Shift the legs to medium heat and grill for about 10 more minutes, bone side down. Flip the chicken again, shift to hot heat, and crisp up the skin for 1 to 2 minutes. Serve immediately.

Crispy Chicken Wings
with Seven-Spice-Powder Marinade

Wings are incredibly popular in Japan, where they're fried, steamed, poached, and, of course, grilled. Called *teba yaki*, grilled chicken wings are prepared in a number of ways and also served skewered, as yakitori. We love them with *shichimi togarashi*, but they're also terrific just grilled with salt.

Serves 4

1/2 cup sesame oil

2 tablespoons shichimi togarashi (page 7)

1/4 cup soy sauce

2 teaspoons salt

2 pounds chicken wings

Whisk together the sesame oil, *shichimi togarashi*, soy sauce, and salt in a bowl to make the marinade. Pour three-fourths of the marinade onto a baking dish or rimmed sheet pan; reserve the rest. Lay the wings in the marinade and flip them 4 times to generously coat all over.

Preheat a grill to high. Grill the wings for about 8 minutes, flipping about every 1 minute and brushing on the reserved marinade after each turn. The wings are ready when they are sizzling and browned. Serve immediately.

Fundamental (But Amazing) Japanese Grilled Chicken

Here's the most basic way to grill chicken, Japanese-style: Bone the flavorful leg meat (leg and thigh) and lightly season with salt. Grill until the chicken just cooks through—that's it. Eat with a dab of green *yuzu kosho* (page 7), if you'd like. With an absolutely pristine piece of *jidori* (or any heirloom breed of chicken), this is about as chicken-y good as it gets. In fact, in the southern city of Miyazaki, a small but chicken-crazed town with hundreds of chicken grill joints, the prized local bird is fast-grilled over flaming coals with the barest of seasonings and served pink inside. Eating chicken this way in America violates culinary orthodoxy, we know, but if you ever have the chance to try the absolutely freshly slaughtered, fast-grilled chicken in Miyazaki, we promise you'll become a believer.

Ginger-Garlic Half Chicken

Preparing half chickens on the grill reveals the beauty of cooking chicken with the bones intact. Even though you're grilling this chicken for 30 minutes, it will turn out tender, incredibly flavorful—and never dry. Thank the bones for that. Grill covered to create radiant heat that will penetrate the thickest parts of the bird and cook it evenly.

Serves 4

1/2 cup soy sauce

2 tablespoons sake

2 tablespoons grated fresh ginger

4 cloves grated garlic

2 teaspoons tobanjan (page 7)

2 tablespoons packed brown sugar

1 teaspoon salt

2 half chickens (3 to 4 pounds total)

Mix together the soy sauce, sake, ginger, garlic, *tobanjan*, brown sugar, and salt in a bowl to make the marinade. Pour three-fourths of the marinade into a baking dish or rimmed sheet pan; reserve the rest. Lay the chicken in the marinade and flip the halves 4 times to generously coat all over. Use a rubber spatula or your hands to make sure all the crevices are well coated. Marinate the chicken halves for 10 minutes, turning once.

Preheat a grill to medium. Grill the chicken, covered, for about 35 minutes. Start by grilling skin side down for about 2 minutes. Flip the chicken and brush on the reserved marinade. Flip the chicken about every 7 minutes, brushing on more marinade after each turn. The chickens are done when very juicy with meat pulling away from the bone. Rest the chicken for 5 minutes, cut into serving pieces, and serve.

Turkey Burger with Quick Barbecue Sauce

Here's Tadashi's take on a turkey burger, Japanese style, accompanied by a quick and easy barbecue sauce. In Japan, hamburger is usually served as "hamburger-steak," that is, a patty served on a plate covered in sauce. You can enjoy your turkey burger this way, too, or—sacrilege—stick it in a bun.

Serves 4

BARBECUE SAUCE

1 tablespoon miso (page 6)

¼ cup ketchup

1 tablespoon mirin

1 tablespoon sake

2 teaspoons sesame oil

TURKEY BURGER

1 pound ground turkey

1 tablespoon red miso (page 6)

2 tablespoons sesame oil

2 teaspoons sake

½ teaspoon sansho (page 7)

¼ cup chopped scallions (white and green parts)

To prepare the sauce, mix together the miso, ketchup, mirin, sake, and 2 teaspoons sesame oil in a bowl. Divide the marinade equally between 2 separate bowls (you'll use half the barbecue sauce for grilling and half for dabbing on the finished burgers). Set aside.

To prepare the burgers, mix together the ground turkey, miso, 1 tablespoon of the sesame oil, sake, *sansho*, and scallions in a large mixing bowl. Knead the meat until it becomes sticky and binds together; divide the mixture into 4 equal parts. For each patty, use your palms (coated with the remaining 1 tablespoon sesame oil to prevent sticking) to roll 1 part into a ball, then flatten the ball by shifting it from hand to hand, until you form a ½-inch-thick patty (patting like this compresses the meat and removes air pockets, which will prevent even heat distribution). Press down in the center of each patty to make an indentation, which prevents the burger from puffing up into a ball as it grills. Place each patty on a piece of aluminum foil to make it easier to transfer to the grill. (Remove the aluminum foil before grilling.)

Preheat a grill to medium. Grill the burgers for about 8 minutes, flipping once, until they're nicely browned. Brush on the barbecue sauce and grill for 1 more minute, flipping once, and brushing on more barbecue sauce after turning. Let the burgers rest for 2 minutes. Spoon the reserved barbecue sauce on top and serve.

Japanese-Style Turkey Pastrami

Like turkey burgers, turkey pastrami is another popular American preparation for the grill, so why not do it Japanese style? This smoky, peppery turkey pastrami is also great cold, in salads, or in a sandwich—perfect leftover food. It also freezes well for up to a month. If you prefer less kick, use less *shichimi togarashi*. Soak the smoking chips so they smolder more slowly. If you're using a gas grill, add all the chips to a smoking pan, then place it in the grill after the grill's been preheated.

Serves 4

2 cups water

1/4 cup soy sauce

1/4 cup Japanese rice vinegar

1 scallion, coarsely chopped

1/2 ounce unpeeled fresh ginger, thinly sliced

3 cloves garlic, crushed

2 tablespoons packed brown sugar

1 teaspoon salt

2 pounds boneless, skinless turkey breast

2 tablespoons shichimi togarashi (page 7)

1 tablespoon sansho (page 7)

2 cups mesquite smoking chips

Mix together 1 cup of the water, soy sauce, vinegar, scallion, ginger, garlic, brown sugar, and salt in a large bowl to make the marinade. Add the turkey breast and let marinate, covered, for 2 days in the refrigerator, turning it once a day. Remove the turkey from the marinade and pat it dry with a paper towel.

Mix together the *shichimi togarashi* and *sansho* in a bowl. Rub this seasoning mixture over the turkey breast, making sure to coat it completely. Combine the mesquite smoking chips with the remaining 1 cup of water in a bowl, soak for 1 hour, then drain.

Set up a grill for indirect heat (medium-low heat; see page 15). Place the turkey as far as you can from the fire side (so the turkey grills on low heat). Grill the turkey, covered, for about 1 hour, turning once. Sprinkle a handful of mesquite chips every 10 minutes over the fire, to smoke. When the turkey is done, it will feel firm when you press down on it with tongs. Allow the turkey to come to room temperature. Slice and serve.

Butterflied Cornish Game Hens with Orange–Soy Sauce Glaze

Despite the fancy name, Cornish game hens are young domesticated chickens, tender and delicious. The citrus and soy sauce marinade gives off a heady, roast-y aroma while grilling. Placing aluminum foil under the birds to finish them, as we describe, protects the birds from burning.

Serves 4

2 Cornish game hens (about 3 pounds)

¼ cup soy sauce

¼ cup freshly squeezed orange juice

2 teaspoons sugar

2 teaspoons grated fresh ginger

1 teaspoon red yuzu kosho (page 7)

½ teaspoon salt

To butterfly the hens, place a hen on a cutting board, breast side down. With a heavy knife, cut out the bird's spine, slicing on both sides of the bone the entire length of the back. Turn the bird over and tap the heel of your knife down the entire length of the breastbone to slightly crack it. Turn the bird over again and flatten it with your palms. The bird is now butterflied. Trim off any excess fat and skin. To tuck in the legs, cut two 1-inch slits in the breast skin by the cavity and fit the ends of the drumsticks into the slits. Now tuck in the wings. Repeat this procedure with the other hen.

Whisk together the soy sauce, orange juice, sugar, ginger, *yuzu kosho*, and salt in a bowl to make the marinade. Pour three-fourths of the marinade into a baking dish or rimmed sheet pan; reserve the rest. Lay the hens in the marinade and flip them 4 times to generously coat all over. Use a rubber spatula or your hands to completely coat all the crevices. Marinate the hens for 30 minutes at room temperature, turning once.

Preheat a grill to medium. Brush and oil the grate well. Grill the game hens, covered, for about 20 minutes. Start with the skin side down for about 2 minutes. Flip the hens and brush on the reserved marinade. Grill for about another 10 minutes. Slide a piece of aluminum foil under the game hens. Grill for about 8 more minutes, flipping 2 more times, and brushing on more marinade after each turn. Use two spatulas to hold the foil down when turning. The birds' thin skin will split, but that's okay; when they're ready, the hens will be browned and sizzling. Test for doneness by cutting a slit into the joint between the thigh and breast; if the juices run clear, the birds are done. Let the game hens rest for about 3 minutes and serve.

Miso-Glazed Quail

Cooking quail with miso (fermented soy bean paste) is a traditional preparation in Japan—the miso mellows the birds' gaminess. "Boneless" quail are typically sold with the body boned, but the bones intact in the legs and wings.

Serves 4

¼ cup plus 1 tablespoon red miso (page 6)

1 tablespoon sake

1 tablespoon mirin

1 tablespoon olive oil

2 teaspoons sansho (page 7), plus more for accent

8 boneless quail (about 3 pounds)

Mix together the miso, sake, mirin, olive oil, and the 2 teaspoons of *sansho* in a bowl to make the marinade. Pour half of the marinade into a baking dish or rimmed sheet pan; reserve the rest. Lay the quail in the marinade and flip them 4 times to generously coat the birds all over. Marinate the quail for 15 minutes at room temperature, turning once.

Preheat a grill to medium heat. Brush and oil the grate well. Grill the quail for about 8 minutes total, starting with the breast side down, and flipping the quail about every 2 minutes, brushing on the reserved marinade after each turn. The birds will become browned and crispy when done. Rest the quail for about 2 minutes. Accent with *sansho* and serve.

Butterflied Hatcho-Miso Squab

Squab is a young pigeon, whose dense, red meat marries perfectly with the dense, powerfully flavored *Hatcho miso*. Grill squab to "rose," like they do in Japan; you want the meat pink inside.

Serves 4

2 pigeons (2 to 2¹/₂ pounds)

¹/₄ cup Hatcho miso (page 7)

¹/₄ cup sake

1 tablespoon mirin

2 teaspoons sesame oil

2 teaspoons shichimi togarashi (page 7), plus more for accent

To butterfly the squab, place one bird on a cutting board, breast side down. With a heavy knife, cut out the bird's spine, slicing on both sides of the bone the entire length of the back. Turn the bird over and tap the heel of your knife down the entire length of the breastbone to slightly crack it. Turn the bird over again and flatten it with your palms. The bird is now butterflied. Trim off any excess fat and skin and cut off the wings at the breast. Rinse the squab thoroughly under cold running water until it's no longer bloody; pat dry with paper towels. Repeat this procedure with the other squab.

To make the marinade, add the miso, sake, mirin, sesame oil, and the 2 teaspoons of *shichimi togarashi* to the jar of a blender. Cover and pulse until smooth, about 1 minute. Pour half of the marinade into a baking dish or rimmed sheet pan; reserve the rest. Lay the squab in the marinade and flip them 4 times to generously coat the birds all over. Marinate the squab for 30 minutes at room temperature, turning once.

Preheat a grill to medium heat. Brush and oil the grate well. Grill the squab, covered, for about 15 minutes total. Start with the breast side down. Flip the squab about every 2 minutes, brushing on the reserved marinade after each turn. After about 10 minutes, slide a piece of aluminum foil under the squab to protect them from burning. Flip and brush on more marinade 2 more times, using two spatulas to hold the foil down while turning, until the birds become nicely lacquered and glossy. Be careful not to grill too long; the squab should be cooked medium-rare (pink inside). Rest the birds for about 3 minutes, accent with *shichimi togarashi*, and serve.

Green Tea–Smoked Duck

We borrow a Chinese technique for infusing an irresistible smoky tea essence into duck, in this case, fragrant Japanese green tea. The breast has a thick layer of fat on the skin; cutting crosshatches into it and sprinkling the bird with salt help the skin get crisp and render fat while grilling. The crosshatches also serve an aesthetic purpose—they make the duck look irresistible when served. If you're using a gas grill, add the all chips and tea to a smoking pan, then place it in the grill after it's been preheated.

Serves 4

$^1/_2$ cup Japanese green tea leaves (*sencha*), plus more for sprinkling

$^1/_2$ cup mesquite smoking chips

$^1/_2$ cup water

2 duck breasts (about $1^1/_4$ pounds)

Salt

Freshly ground black pepper

Combine the green tea, smoking chips, and $^1/_2$ cup water in a bowl. Soak for 1 hour. All the water should be absorbed by the tea and chips, but if there's any water left, drain it off.

Trim off excess fat from the duck breasts and cut cross-hatches into the duck's skin, about $^1/_8$ inch deep and $^1/_4$ inch apart. Season the duck breasts with salt and pepper all over. Let the duck rest for 30 minutes at room temperature. Wipe off any moisture that appears on the surface of the breasts with paper towels.

Set up a grill for indirect heat (medium-low heat; see page 15). Place the duck on the indirect side, skin side down, as close as you can to the fire side (so the duck grills on medium-low heat). Grill the duck, covered, for about 30 minutes. Sprinkle a handful of green tea leaves over the fire every 5 minutes, to smoke. Flip the duck after about 20 minutes. For the final minute of grilling, flip the duck again (skin side down now) and shift it directly over the coals to crisp the skin. When the duck is ready, the skin will be browned, the meat ruddy, and all will have a wonderful tea-smoke fragrance. Let the duck rest for 5 minutes. Slice and serve.

FISH AND SEAFOOD

JAPAN IS AN ISLAND NATION blessed with the world's greatest fisheries; seafood has always been central to the diet there, and fish is honored as a traditional festive dish. Hundreds of varieties of sea life are harvested in Japan, which is home to the world's largest wholesale fish market and over 200,000 fishermen (for a country the size of California). The hallmarks of Japanese fish cooking are simple and delicious flavors and an obsession with the clean, natural taste of seafood—you're not going to find fish drowned in heavy sauces. Eating seafood in its purest state—raw—is a foun-dation of the cuisine (think sushi and sashimi), but so is grill-ing fish. While we typically prefer fillets of fish in America, in Japan every part of the fish is savored, from the head, gills, guts, bones, and fins all the way down to the tail. We encour-age you to try our whole-fish grilling to discover the incred-ible taste of parts you might not have encountered before. In this chapter, we share traditional preparations, like classic salt-grilling, as well as more contemporary interpretations. The dishes are all simple, fast to prepare, and incredibly tasty; we hope you try them all.

Grilling Fish Basics

A few things to keep in mind when grilling fish:

- **A well-oiled cooking grate is essential. If you don't preheat, brush clean, then lube that grate up, your fish will abso-lutely stick. If you do preheat, brush, and oil, grilling fish will be a pleasure, we promise.**

- **One or two thin fish spatulas with a 6-inch or so long blade (one in each hand is best) are key for turning fish without breaking them.**

- **Salt your fish before grilling. Why? Salting cures and concentrates the flavor in fish and draws out water from the flesh, making the fish denser and easier to handle on the grill. Our recipes call for salting for various lengths of time, depending on the size and type of fish. Salt all fish at room temperature.**

- **Finally, you don't need a so-called fish grilling basket. We don't use them.**

Salt-Grilled Head-On Shrimp

Salt-grilling these big shrimp crisps up the head and shell and turns the flesh tender and succulent. Make sure to eat the whole delicious thing—the flesh as well as the head, tail, and shell. Don't be afraid to suck the juices out of the head, too (might not be pretty, but incredibly good). All types of large shrimp work great, including Gulf, White Tiger, Maya, and New Caledonia Blue.

Serves 4

12 large unshelled, head-on shrimp, about 1 pound

Salt

1 lime, quartered (optional)

To clean and devein the shrimp, first trim off the spear-like protrusion on the shell of each shrimp's head. Cut an incision lengthwise along the back of each shrimp to reveal its dark-colored digestive tract (the "vein") and scrape it out with the tip of your knife. Rinse the shrimp under cold running water and pat them dry with paper towels. Lightly season the shrimp with salt all over.

Preheat a grill to medium-hot. Brush the cooking grate clean and oil it well. Grill the shrimp about 1 1/2 minutes per side; when the shrimp are ready, the shells will turn pink, and juice will bubble out of the heads. Serve immediately. Squeeze a little lime on the shrimp and eat everything—the flesh, shell, and head.

Shioyaki

Salt-grilling—*shioyaki*—is as old as Japanese culture itself, with fish skewered upright on stakes and grilled in the *irori* (open hearth) since ancient times. With certain kinds of fish, like *ayu*, a Japanese river fish, this rustic style of grilling can be elevated to a high art; a skilled cook can tease out the fish's intrinsic flavor with just salt and the fish's position on the fire. The trick to salt-grilling is to crisp the outside but leave the inside tender, moist, and juicy. Try this method with salmon, trout, sea bass, and more. To eat *shioyaki* the Japanese way: drip soy sauce onto a mound of *daikon oroshi* (page 73) and eat together with the fish; dip the fish into ponzu (page 69) mixed with *daikon oroshi* or *momiji oroshi* (see page 73); squeeze lemon or lime over the fish; or do nothing—and savor the salt-grilled fish on its own, like they do with *ayu* in Japan.

Salt-Grilled Whole Sardines

If you can get your hands on really fresh sardines, do like they do in Japan—grill 'em and eat 'em, guts, heads, and all. Japanese enjoy the cooked guts for their bitter, complex flavor, and once you try them this way, we're sure you will, too. (You can, of course, grill the sardines already gutted and cleaned, if you prefer.) Grilling softens the small bones in the fish; pull out the spine before eating.

Serves 4

8 extremely fresh sardines (about 1 pound), scaled but not gutted

Salt

1 lime, quartered (optional)

Pour cold water in a small bowl and dip the sardines' tails in the water. Pack salt on the tails to prevent them from burning (the salt will stick to the wet tails). Lightly season the rest of the sardines with salt all over.

Preheat a grill to medium-hot. Brush the cooking grate clean and oil it well. Grill the sardines until the skin gets crispy and the fish becomes firm to the touch, about 5 minutes. If you're grilling the sardines without gutting them (the way we prefer), the stomachs may break open, but that's okay. Serve immediately. Squeeze a little lime on the sardines and eat the heads; the small bones (they soften during grilling); and, of course, the guts.

Forget Fishiness

Japanese love all kinds of seafood, including strong-flavored oily fish like mackerel, herring, sardines, and anchovies that many of us here shy away from. Japanese ingredients paired with fish, even oily ones, even eaten raw, what make them so delicious. Chemical compounds found in traditional fermented ingredients like miso, soy sauce, mirin, and sake naturally balance and diminish a pronounced sense of "fishiness" in fish. This palliative effect has been proven by modern science, but Japanese cooks have known this, empirically, for centuries. So go ahead and grill fish in our recipes that you might not have tried before; we guarantee the Japanese flavors we pair with them will blow you away and make these fish welcoming and incredibly delicious.

Ponzu

Ponzu is a fundamental flavoring sauce in Japanese cuisine, with countless uses and countless ready-made varieties available at Japanese markets. But none of these bottled versions compare to the taste of ponzu that you make yourself. As you'll see from this recipe, making ponzu from scratch is fast and easy. Typically, ponzu is paired with *daikon oroshi* or *momiji oroshi* (page 73); the grated daikon adds its own fresh flavor and helps the sauce adhere to foods. Ponzu works perfectly as a citrusy, vinegary dipping sauce for any kind of grilled foods, from mushrooms and vegetables to fish, chicken, or meat. Kombu, naturally preserved kelp, and katsuobushi, dried shaved bonito flakes (a type of tuna), are fundamental Japanese ingredients that infuse this sauce with loads of umami and flavor. Use a combination of citrus juices, bottled pure yuzu juice, or just lemon juice, which works fine, too.

Makes about 1¹/₂ cups

3 tablespoons sake

1 tablespoon mirin

¹/₂ cup soy sauce

¹/₄ cup citrus juice (any combination of lemon, lime, grapefruit, and orange juice—preferably, at least half lemon juice)

¹/₄ cup rice vinegar

¹/₄ cup water

1 (6-inch) piece kombu

¹/₄ cup (about ¹/₈ ounce) tightly packed dried, shaved bonito flakes (*katsuobushi*)

Add the sake and mirin to a small saucepan and bring to a boil over high heat. Boil for 1 minute, remove from heat, and let the liquid come to room temperature.

In a bowl, stir together the soy sauce, citrus juice, vinegar, the ¹/₄ cup water, the sake mixture, kombu, and bonito flakes. Cover loosely with plastic wrap and let the mixture steep in the refrigerator for 12 hours, or overnight. Strain the ponzu through a cheesecloth or fine sieve; gently squeeze to press out the liquid. The ponzu will keep in the refrigerator for 2 weeks.

Whole Red Snapper with Ponzu

Salt-grilled fish with ponzu, simple and elegant, is a signature dish of Japanese cuisine. Grilling the fish with the bones intact adds flavor, succulence, and juiciness to the flesh. If you prefer, you can cut off the head, but we love its tender parts, including the cheek and the insides. You can also use this grilling technique with whole sea bass, bronzini, sea bream, porgy, small grouper, dorade (also called Mediterranean sea bream), or other white-fleshed fish.

Serves 4

2 whole red snappers (about 2 pounds), scaled, gutted, and cleaned

Salt

1/2 cup momiji oroshi (page 73)

1/2 cup finely chopped scallions (white and green parts)

1 cup ponzu (page 69), divided between 4 small dipping bowls

Lightly season the fish with salt all over, including the cavities. Let the fish rest for 30 minutes at room temperature. Wipe off moisture that accumulates on the surface of the fish with paper towels. Cut a 1/2-inch-deep slit lengthwise along the centerline of each fish, from head to tail. Do this on both sides; the cuts will help the fish cook faster and make it easier to flake off the grilled flesh.

To make the dipping sauce, divide the *momiji oroshi* and scallions between the 4 bowls of ponzu; set aside.

Preheat a grill to medium-hot. Brush the cooking grate clean and oil it well. Grill the fish about 5 minutes per side. Flip the snappers with care—gently turn them with a fish spatula so they don't break apart. When the fish are ready, you'll see juice bubbling from the back, and if you peek inside the cavity, you'll see that the spine and flesh near it will have turned white. Serve the fish immediately, accompanied by the ponzu dipping sauce.

Skewering Fish

With traditional Japanese grilling, ingredients are first skewered with skewers of various sizes and grilled over charcoal—but usually without a cooking grate. This gives the cook total control over the foods, to angle them in three dimensions to grill perfectly, so the skin turns fragrant and crisp, and the flesh, succulent and tender. Skewering and grilling in Japan reach their finest expression with fish. Whole river fish are trussed with a technique called *odori gushi*—dancing skewering—in which the fish are threaded to look like they're swimming upstream. With whole ocean fish, this presentation is called *uneri gushi*—wave skewering. For both methods, only one side of the fish is skewered, and the tail and fins are coated in a thick layer of salt so they don't burn off. The result is an arresting aesthetic presentation which only accentuates the taste. *Tsuma ore gushi*—tucked under skewering, a reference to the way kimonos are tucked when walking—is used for fillets of fish to keep them moist. For small fish like anchovies, *ori-gushi*—fan skewering—holds a number of them in place with a trio of skewers spread out like a fan. *Mezashi*—"stick in the eye"—is just that, a skewer pushed through the the eyes of small fish so they all can be grilled and angled together at the same time (in this case, on a wire grid).

Daikon Oroshi and Momiji Oroshi

Raw grated daikon—a radish that looks like a giant white carrot—paired with soy sauce or ponzu is a classic Japanese accompaniment for grilled fish and other ingredients. The grated daikon offers a refreshing counterpoint to these foods and also helps you digest oily ingredients (like oily fish) with its natural digestive enzymes. The daikon is typically prepared two ways, as either *daikon oroshi* or *momiji oroshi*.

Daikon oroshi simply means grated daikon. Peel the thick skin to expose the translucent flesh and grate with either a specialized Japanese daikon grater or a box grater; gently squeeze out excess liquid (but don't squeeze totally dry). The spicy-tasting tip of the daikon is best for grating. To accompany grilled fish, drip soy sauce onto *daikon oroshi* and eat together with the fish, or mix *daikon oroshi* together with ponzu (page 69), which also thickens the thin ponzu and makes it easier to adhere, and eat together with the fish.

Momiji oroshi, or "red maple leaf" grated daikon, is daikon grated together with whole dried Japanese chilies, hence the evocative name. To make about ½ cup: thickly peel 1 pound daikon and quarter the daikon lengthwise. Soak 16 whole chilies in hot water for 5 minutes. Use a chopstick to poke a hole into the flat end of each daikon piece and stuff a chili into it, using the chopstick as a plunger. Grate the two together with a fine grater. When you've used up the chili, poke another hole in the remaining daikon and stuff another chili into it; repeat with all the chilies and daikon. Mix the daikon-chili mixture well and gently squeeze out excess liquid (but don't squeeze totally dry). *Momiji oroshi* adds heat, of course, in addition to the goodness of daikon, and is typically mixed with ponzu to eat with grilled fish and other foods.

Yuzu Kosho Marinade

We love yuzu kosho, an irresistible and super aromatic marriage of fiery chilies, salt, and tangy Japanese yuzu citrus zest and juice. Used in this marinade, it adds incredible savoriness and citrus-y heat to white-fleshed fish, chicken, and pork. Quick and easy to prepare, it's one of our essential marinades for grilling. (This marinade also works great with pan-sautéed or oven-baked fish, chicken, and pork.)

Makes about ³/₄ cup

2 tablespoons red yuzu kosho (page 7)

2 tablespoons soy sauce

¹/₂ cup olive oil

Whisk together the *yuzu kosho*, soy sauce, and olive oil in a bowl. This marinade will keep in the refrigerator for up to 2 weeks. Just mix again before using it.

Yuzu Kosho Bronzini

Peppery, tangy, and savory, yuzu kosho marinade will liven up any fillet of white-fleshed fish, like this bronzini (also called Mediterranean sea bass). Try this marinade with fillets of flounder, pink snapper, turbot, and sea bass, too.

Serves 4

8 bronzini fillets (about 1 1/2 pounds)

Salt

1/2 cup Yuzu Kosho Marinade (page 74)

Lightly season the bronzini fillets with salt all over. Let them rest for 1 hour at room temperature. Wipe off moisture that accumulates on the surface of the fish with paper towels.

Reserve 2 tablespoons of the marinade and set aside. Pour the remaining marinade onto a baking dish or rimmed sheet pan. Lay the bronzini fillets in the marinade and gently turn them 4 times to generously coat all over.

Preheat a grill to medium-hot. Brush the cooking grate clean and oil it well. Place the bronzini on the grill skin side down and grill about 1 minute per side. The thin fillets cook quickly; the flesh will become firm and turn white when ready. Remove from the grill, brush the reserved marinade on the fillets, and serve immediately.

Yuzu Kosho Scallops

Dense, delicious sea scallops work great on the grill; they keep their shape and are easy to handle. But be careful when turning them, so they don't fall through the grate.

Serves 4

1/2 cup Yuzu Kosho Marinade (page 74)

20 sea scallops (about 1 1/2 pounds)

Reserve 2 tablespoons of the marinade and set aside. Pour the remaining marinade into a baking dish or rimmed sheet pan. Lay the scallops in the marinade and gently turn them 4 times to generously coat all sides.

Preheat a grill to medium-hot. Brush the cooking grate clean and oil it well. Grill the scallops about 2 minutes on each side. They'll turn from translucent to white and become firm and juicy when they're done. Right before you pull them off the grill, dab the reserved marinade on top of each scallop. Serve immediately.

Garlic–Yuzu Kosho Shrimp

Yuzu kosho also pairs nicely with shrimp. Here we add grated garlic for additional heat and flavor. We use skewers here, but you can also grill the shrimp without them; just lay the shrimp on a wire grid (also called a vegetable grid), so they don't fall through the cooking grate.

Serves 4

16 shrimp (16/20 count), about 1 pound, shelled, cleaned, and deveined

¾ cup Yuzu Kosho Marinade (page 74)

3 cloves garlic, grated

Prepare 4 skewers with 4 shrimp each (see "How to Skewer Yakitori," page 25). Curl the shrimp so the both the body and tails are skewered.

Mix together the marinade and grated garlic in a bowl. Reserve ¼ cup of the marinade and set aside. Pour the remaining marinade into a baking dish or rimmed sheet pan. Lay the skewers in the marinade and gently turn them 4 times to coat all over.

Preheat a grill to hot heat. Grill the shrimp until they become bright pink, about 2 minutes per side. Brush on the reserved marinade after turning the shrimp. Serve immediately.

Swordfish Teriyaki

We use this original style of teriyaki sauce to give grilled fish an intense savory flavor and aroma plus a glossy lacquered sheen (for more on teriyaki, see "Grilled Chicken Breast Teriyaki," page 50). In Japan this dish is typically prepared with yellowtail, but here we use swordfish, which is just as good and easier to find. You can also substitute any dense, meaty fish like shark, mahi mahi, or salmon. Finally, if you want to experiment with other flavors, try spiking the teriyaki with a bit of dried or chopped fresh dill, rosemary, thyme, or tarragon.

Serves 4

1/4 cup plus 2 tablespoons soy sauce

2 tablespoons sake

1/4 cup mirin

1 tablespoon sugar

4 swordfish steaks (1/2 to 3/4 inch thick), skinned, about 2 pounds

Sansho (page 7), for accent

Add the 1/4 cup soy sauce, sake, mirin, and sugar to a saucepan and bring it to a boil over medium heat. Boil for 1 minute, remove from the heat, and let the marinade come to room temperature.

Brush the remaining 2 tablespoons of soy sauce on all sides of the swordfish steaks. Reserve 1/4 cup of the marinade and set aside. Pour the remaining marinade into a baking dish or rimmed sheet pan. Lay the swordfish steaks in the marinade and gently turn them 4 times to generously coat all over. Let the swordfish marinate for 15 minutes.

Preheat a grill to medium-hot. Brush the cooking grate clean and oil it well. Grill the swordfish for about 6 minutes for medium-rare: Start by grilling the fish for about 2 minutes on each side. Flip the swordfish and brush on the reserved marinade. Grill the swordfish for about 2 more minutes, flipping every 30 seconds and brushing on more marinade after each turn. The swordfish will turn a rich honey color as it grills, but be very careful not to burn; if it starts to blacken, pull the fish off the grill. Accent with sansho and serve immediately.

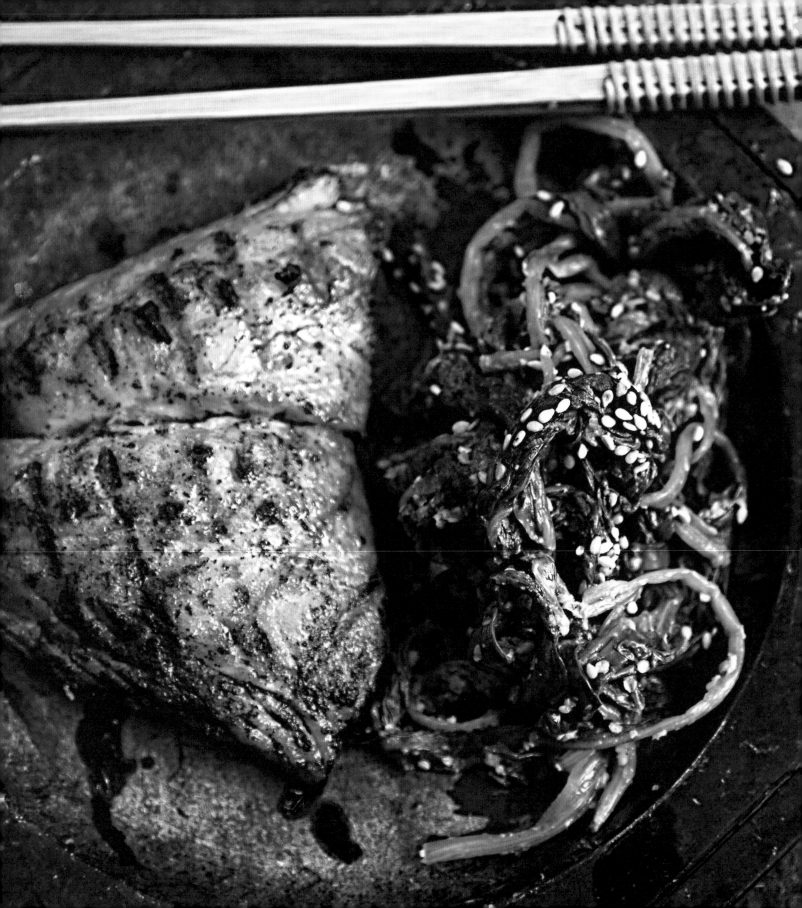

Salmon with Shiso Pesto

This contemporary salmon dish has long been a crowd pleaser at Matsuri, Tadashi's Japanese restaurant in New York City. For his pesto, Tadashi substitutes the traditional basil for the Japanese herb shiso and adds a touch of soy sauce for a savory flavor.

Serves 4

2 pounds salmon fillet, cut into 4 pieces

Salt

2 bunches shiso leaves (about 20 leaves), thinly sliced

1/2 cup olive oil

1 tablespoon soy sauce

Lightly season the salmon fillets with salt on all sides. Let them rest at room temperature for 30 minutes. Wipe off moisture that accumulates on the surface of the fish with paper towels.

Add the shiso leaves, olive oil, soy sauce, and salt to the jar of a blender, cover, and pulse until the pesto is smooth, about 1 minute. Reserve 2 tablespoons of the pesto and set aside. Pour the remaining marinade into a baking dish or rimmed sheet pan. Lay the salmon fillets in the pesto and gently turn them 4 times to generously coat all over.

Preheat a grill to medium-hot. Brush the cooking grate clean and oil it well. Grill the salmon for about 6 minutes for medium-rare (8 minutes for well done), turning once. If the salmon is more than 1 inch thick, grill it for about 2 minutes top and bottom and about 1 minute on each side. Right before you pull the fillets off the grill, dab the reserved marinade on top. Serve immediately.

Tuna with Avocado-Wasabi Puree

Here's another popular preparation from Matsuri, Tadashi's restaurant—rich, creamy avocado meets dense, intense tuna, with the wasabi and lime juice adding heat and bite. Use only sushi grade tuna for this recipe (yellowfin or bigeye [ahi] tuna are great choices) and perfectly ripe avocados. Allow the fish to come to room temperature before grilling, and grill quickly—we like our tuna cooked rare, as we explain in the method. If you prefer, grill the fish for 3 minutes for medium-rare or 4 minutes for medium, but not more than that; if you over-cook tuna, it turns tough and rubbery.

Serves 4

2 avocados, pitted, peeled, and cut into small chunks

1 tablespoon wasabi

1 tablespoon freshly squeezed lime juice

1 teaspoon salt

2 tablespoons chopped fresh chives (you can substitute finely chopped scallions)

1/2 cup Garlic-Soy Sauce Marinade (page 103)

4 tuna steaks (about 2 pounds), about 3/4 inch thick

Add the avocados, wasabi, lime juice, salt, and chives to a bowl; mash the ingredients together with a fork; set aside.

Pour the garlic–soy sauce marinade into a baking dish or rimmed sheet pan. Lay the tuna steaks in the marinade and gently flip them 4 times until the fish is coated all over.

Preheat a grill to medium-hot. Brush the cooking grate clean and oil it well. Grill the tuna quickly, about 2 minutes, turning once. You want to just sear the surface and quickly caramelize the marinade. The tuna should be rare to almost raw inside. Remove from the grill, spoon the avocado puree on top of the tuna, and serve immediately.

Mako Shark with Scallion Oil

This scallion oil is intensely aromatic and irresistible and will add flavor and a touch of heat to the shark. Grill the shark to medium-rare so it stays moist and juicy. You can use the scallion oil with any dense fleshed fish, including swordfish, mahi mahi, salmon, or yellowtail.

Serves 4

¹/₂ cup coarsely chopped scallions (white and green parts)

¹/₂ cup sesame oil

2 tablespoons soy sauce

1 teaspoon salt

1 teaspoon tobanjan (page 7)

2 pounds mako shark (about ¹/₂ inch thick), cut into 4 steaks

Add the scallions, sesame oil, soy sauce, salt, and *tobanjan* to the jar of a blender; cover and pulse until the scallions incorporate into the oil, about 1 minute. It's okay if bits of scallion are visible. Reserve ¹/₄ cup of the scallion oil and set aside. Pour the remaining scallion oil onto a baking dish or rimmed sheet pan. Lay the shark steaks in the scallion oil and gently turn them 4 times to generously coat all over. Let the shark steaks marinate for 15 minutes.

Preheat a grill to medium-hot. Brush the cooking grate clean and oil it well. Grill the shark for about 6 minutes for medium-rare this way: Start by grilling the fish for about 2 minutes per side. Flip the shark and brush on the reserved marinade. Grill the steaks about 2 more minutes, flipping every 30 seconds and brushing on more marinade after each turn. Serve immediately.

Mahi Mahi
with Sesame–Soy Sauce Dipping Sauce

Here mahi mahi is simply salt-grilled to succulent perfection; you accent it, as you desire, by dipping into this fragrant sesame sauce. The sake and mirin in the sauce are first boiled to evaporate the alcohol found in these two liquids, so they add body, but not sharpness. This dipping sauce also works well with other dense-fleshed fish.

Serves 4

2 pounds mahi mahi fillet (1 to 1¹/₂ inches thick), cut into 4 pieces

Salt

¹/₂ cup sake

¹/₄ cup mirin

2 tablespoons soy sauce

3 tablespoons ground sesame seed (buy ground seed or grind whole seed with a spice grinder or clean coffee grinder; see Spinach with Ground Sesame, page 169)

1 teaspoon shichimi togarashi (page 7)

Lightly season the mahi mahi with salt on both sides. Let the fish rest for 15 minutes at room temperature. Wipe off moisture that accumulates on the surface of the fish with paper towels. Lightly season the mahi mahi again with salt on both sides.

Add the sake and mirin to a small saucepan and bring it to a boil over medium heat. Boil for 1 minute to evaporate the alcohol. Remove from the heat and let the liquid come to room temperature. To make the dipping sauce, whisk together the cooled sake–mirin mixture, soy sauce, sesame seed, and *shichimi togarashi* in a bowl. Divide the sauce between 4 small dipping bowls and set aside.

Preheat a grill to medium-hot. Grill the mahi mahi until it's nicely seared and juicy on the outside, about 3 minutes per side. Serve immediately with the dipping sauce.

Hot-Oil Halibut

This dish is inspired by Chinese cuisine, where flavored, aromatic hot oil is often poured over steamed fish. This hot oil method also works great with grilled fish, and is a perfect vehicle for livening up fillet of halibut. Be careful when adding the sake and the soy sauce to the hot oil; pour them into the oil in one shot, instead of dripping them in, so the oil doesn't splash. Use a small cast-iron or other fireproof skillet to make the hot oil so you can reheat it directly on the grill just before serving.

Serves 4

2 pounds halibut fillet (1 to 1½ inches thick), cut into 4 pieces

Salt

½ cup sesame oil

2 tablespoons finely chopped fresh ginger

¼ cup finely chopped scallion (white and green parts)

¼ cup sake

2 tablespoons soy sauce

1 teaspoon shichimi togarashi (page 7)

Lightly season the halibut fillets with salt all over. Let them cure for 30 minutes at room temperature. Wipe off moisture that accumulates on the surface of the fish with paper towels.

While the fish is curing, add the sesame oil, ginger, and scallions to a small fireproof skillet and place it over medium heat. As soon as the oil starts bubbling and the ginger begins to turn golden, about 2 minutes, carefully pour in the sake and the soy sauce in one shot (if you drip it in, the oil might splash up). Sprinkle in the *shichimi togarashi*. Once the liquid comes to a boil, turn off the heat. Carefully transfer the skillet with the hot oil to a work surface beside your grill.

Preheat a grill to medium-hot. Brush the cooking grate clean and oil it well. Grill the halibut for about 8 minutes, turning once. Be careful when turning the fillets, which are delicate and can break apart; use 2 fish spatulas to gently flip them. When done, transfer to a platter or plate and let the fish rest for 2 minutes. While the fish is resting, place the skillet with the hot oil directly on the grill to reheat, for about 2 minutes. Pour the hot oil over the fillets and serve.

Grilled Lobster with Ponzu Brown Butter

The fierce countenance of lobster may have inspired the Japanese name for the grilled version of this crustacean: *onigara yaki*, or "devil shell" grill. Japanese—like many Americans—savor the lobster's tomalley (its green-colored liver), and we certainly recommend eating the tomalley, eggs, and every other part of the lobster. But if you're so inclined, push all that aside and focus on the delicate lobster meat, which we accent with the citrusy ponzu brown butter.

Serves 4

½ cup unsalted butter

½ cup Ponzu (page 69)

1 tablespoon sake

½ teaspoon red yuzu kosho (page 7)

4 live lobsters, about 1 to 1¼ pounds each

Add the butter to a small saucepan and melt over medium heat. When the butter froths, cook for about 2 minutes more, until you see brown bits forming. Add the ponzu, sake, and *yuzu kosho* and stir together the ingredients. When the mixture boils, cook for 30 seconds more. Remove from the heat and set aside.

To prepare the lobsters, place 1 lobster on a cutting board and kill it with a heavy knife by cutting the lobster in half as follows: Grab the head and cut it in half lengthwise; then, holding the split head, cut the tail in half lengthwise. Hit the claws with the back of your knife to crack them, so the flesh inside cooks faster. Repeat with the remaining lobsters.

Preheat a grill to medium. Grill the lobsters for about 3 minutes per side, starting with the flesh side down. When the lobsters are ready, the flesh will be white and toasted, and the shell will turn bright red. Serve the lobsters with the melted ponzu butter on the side or pour the butter sauce over them.

Squid with Ginger–Soy Sauce Marinade

Grilled squid—*yaki ika*—is a fixture of street fairs, shrine festivals, and pushcart vendors. Its phenomenal soy sauce fragrance makes it almost impossible to pass by without wanting one.

Serves 4

¹/₂ cup soy sauce

2 tablespoons grated fresh ginger

3 tablespoons mirin

1 pound small squid (bodies and tentacles), cleaned

Mix together the soy sauce, ginger, and mirin in a large bowl to make the marinade. Reserve ¹/₂ cup of the marinade and set aside. Lay the squid in the remaining liquid, gently turning 4 times to coat all over. Marinate the squid for 10 minutes at room temperature, turning once.

Preheat a grill to hot. Grill the squid for about 4 minutes (5 minutes if they're larger than 1 ounce apiece). Every 30 seconds flip the squid and brush on the reserved marinade. The squid will turn from translucent to white when they're ready, becoming tender and releasing a rich aroma. Be careful not to overcook; squid turns rubbery if grilled too long. Serve immediately.

Littleneck Clams with Soy Sauce

Grilled clams are an iconic Tokyo dish, especially in the old fisherman neighborhoods that ring Tokyo Bay, which was once teeming with shellfish. Called *yakihama* (*hamaguri* are a kind of large clam available in Japan), this cooking tradition reaches back hundreds of years. The littleneck clams that are available here are a good substitute. *Mitsuba* is a fresh-tasting Japanese herb available at Japanese markets. If you can't find it, you can also use cilantro or flat-leaf parsely.

Serves 4

24 littleneck clams (larger ones are better)

$1/2$ cup soy sauce

$1/4$ cup sake

$1/4$ cup chopped mitsuba, for garnish

Rinse the clams under cold running water to remove any caked-on sand or mud. Whisk together the soy sauce and sake in a bowl to make the marinade; set aside.

Preheat a grill to medium-hot. Place the clams directly on the grill. After about 2 minutes they'll start to open. (Discard any clams that don't open.) Using 2 pairs of tongs, or tongs and a large spoon, carefully pry the shells open completely. Pour about 1 teaspoon of the marinade over each clam. As soon as the clams begin to froth and boil, about 1 minute more, pull them off the grill. Make sure not to overcook the clams or they'll get rubbery. Garnish with the *mitsuba* and serve.

Foil-Baked Whole Trout
with Lemon–Soy Sauce Butter

Using foil is a great way to prepare delicate fish like trout that would ordinarily fall apart on the grill. The foil also traps the juices and flavors of this dish and lets them mingle instead of drip off. Once you finish eating the top half of the fish, pull the head off and the spine will pull away, too, letting you tuck into the bottom half. This trout is great cold, too. Leftovers, anyone? (Don't eat the sliced lemons, they're for flavor.)

Serves 4

4 whole rainbow trout ($^3/_4$ to 1 pound each)

Salt

4 tablespoons ($^1/_2$ stick) unsalted butter, thinly sliced, plus 2 tablespoons (for smearing)

2 lemons, thinly sliced

$^1/_4$ cup soy sauce

Yuzu kosho (page 7), optional

Lightly season the trout with salt all over, including the cavity. Let the trout rest for 30 minutes at room temperature. Wipe off moisture that accumulates on the surface of the fish with paper towels. Cut about a $^1/_4$-inch-deep slit lengthwise along the rainbow-colored strip (the centerline) on the sides of each fish, from head to tail. Do this on both sides; the cut will help the trout cook faster and absorb flavor.

Cut four 12- by 18-inch pieces of aluminum foil, fold them in half so the shiny side is on the outside, and place them on a work surface. For each trout, smear a thin film of butter on the center of the foil the size of the fish. Lay a row of lemon slices on the butter and place a trout over them. Top the fish with another row of lemon slices, then place butter slices on the lemon. Pour 1 tablespoon of the soy sauce over the fish. Fold over the long sides of the foil and fold and pinch the ends closed; it's okay if the foil package isn't airtight (this will allow steam to escape when grilling).

Preheat a grill to medium-hot. Grill the trout in their foil packets about 6 minutes per side, starting with the seam side first. When it's time to turn them, you'll see butter and juices dripping out of the foil pouches. Transfer each trout to its own plate and carefully unwrap the fish (watch out for escaping steam). Drizzle 1 teaspoon of the soy sauce over each fish and dab with *yuzu kosho*. Serve immediately.

Catfish in Bamboo Leaf

What's wonderful about wrapping catfish in bamboo leaves is that the bamboo aroma and flavor infuse the fish, giving it a sublime smoky flavor without actually smoking. You can usually find fresh bamboo leaves at Asian markets. This technique also works great with trout, pike, and bronzini.

Serves 4

4 catfish fillets (about 1 1/2 pounds)

Salt

1/4 cup olive oil

8 fresh (not dried) bamboo leaves

2 teaspoons sake

2 teaspoons soy sauce

1 tablespoon green yuzu kosho (page 7)

Lightly season the catfish fillets with salt all over. Let them rest for 15 minutes at room temperature. Wipe off moisture that accumulates on the surface of the fish with paper towels. With a brush or your fingers, coat both sides of the fillets with olive oil.

Cut four 12-inch squares of aluminum foil, fold them in half so the shiny side is on the outside, and place them on a work surface. For each fillet lay a bamboo leaf on the foil and coat it with olive oil. Place a catfish fillet on the bamboo leaf. Drizzle 1/2 teaspoon of the sake and 1/2 teaspoon of the soy sauce on the fillet, and dab with 1/4 teaspoon *yuzu kosho*. Mix together the remaining sake, soy sauce, and *yuzu kosho* and gently apply it with a pastry brush or your fingers to the surface of the fish. Cover the catfish with another bamboo leaf. Fold the foil over and fold and pinch the ends closed; it's okay if the foil package isn't airtight (this will allow steam to escape when grilling).

Preheat a grill to hot. Grill the catfish for 3 minutes per side; the fillets cook through quickly. Transfer each catfish to its own plate and carefully unwrap the fish (watch out for escaping steam). Serve immediately.

Cedar Plank–Grilled Arctic Char

Grilling fish on a cedar plank adds incredible smoky flavor and also means the fish will never stick to the grate, a plus. The wasabi and ginger add complexity to this easy to prepare dish. The skin *will* stick to the plank during grilling, but that's okay. Just leave it on the plank, and enjoy the rest of the fish. You can also use this method with salmon and trout. Remember that the cedar planks must soak in water overnight before using.

Serves 4

4 ($^1/_8$-inch-thick) cedar planks, for grilling (each approximately 8 to 10 inches long)

Olive oil

2 tablespoons wasabi

2 tablespoons sugar

1 tablespoon soy sauce

1 tablespoon grated fresh ginger

4 arctic char fillets, about 2 pounds

Salt

Soak the cedar planks in water for 12 hours, or overnight. Blot the planks dry with paper towels. Soak another paper towel with olive oil and use it to coat one side of each plank. Set aside. Mix together the wasabi, sugar, 2 tablespoons of the olive oil, soy sauce, and ginger in a bowl to make the marinade. Set aside.

Season the arctic char with salt all over. Let the fish rest for 15 minutes at room temperature. Wipe off moisture that accumulates on the surface of the fish with paper towels. Lay each fish on the oiled side of a cedar plank, skin side down. Generously brush marinade on top of the fish.

Preheat a grill to medium-hot. Place the fish-topped cedar planks on the grill. Grill, covered, until the flesh begins splitting on top and the marinade is bubbling, about 8 minutes. The planks may burn a little, but that's okay. Use a fish spatula to ease the char off the planks and serve immediately.

Smoked Trout with Wasabi Sour Cream

Smoked trout is delicious hot off the grill or served at room temperature, with the wasabi sour cream adding a bit of heat and richness. You can refrigerate the grilled trout for a week or freeze it for up to one month. If you're using a gas grill, add all the chips to a smoking pan, then place it in the grill after the grill's been preheated.

Serves 4

4 trout (about 1¹/₂ pounds), butterflied (ask your fish market to do this)

Salt

1 cup mesquite smoking chips

1 cup water

¹/₂ cup wasabi sour cream (page 109 bone-in rib-eye recipe)

Season the trout with salt all over and let the fish cure for 1 hour at room temperature. Wipe off any moisture on the surface of the fish with paper towels.

Combine the mesquite soaking chips with the 1 cup of water in a bowl and soak them for 1 hour. Drain before using.

Set up a grill for indirect heat (medium-low heat; see page 15). Brush and oil the grate well. Sprinkle a handful of mesquite chips over the fire and place the trout as far as you can from the fire side (so the fish grills on low heat), skin side down. For each side, grill 4 minutes covered, then 1 minute uncovered to brown. Sprinkle more mesquite chips over the fire when you turn the trout. Uncover the grill and shift the trout over the coals for 1 minute to brown it, flipping once. Place a dollop of wasabi sour cream on top of each fish and serve immediately.

Salt-Cured Salmon

Salt-cured salmon, *shiojake*, is a classic Japanese ingredient and a traditional New Year's gift. We love firm, meaty wild salmon like sockeye, Copper River, or Alaskan king for this technique. Eat the salmon with *daikon oroshi* (page 73) and soy sauce or with just a squeeze of fresh lemon juice. Crumble leftover salmon on rice or rice porridge or pack it in the center of *onigiri* (rice balls, page 156).

Serves 4

2 pounds salmon fillet (1 inch thick)

2 tablespoons coarse sea salt or kosher salt

1/2 cup Daikon Oroshi (page 73), for accent

2 tablespoons soy sauce, for accent

Choose a baking dish or rimmed sheet pan large enough to hold the salmon fillets in one layer (you can cut the fillets in half, if necessary). Line the baking dish or sheet pan with 3 layers of paper towels. Generously coat the salmon with sea salt all over; lay the fish, skin side down, on the paper towels. Let the salmon cure at room temperature for 2 hours. Wipe off the moisture and salt that has accumulated on the surface of the fish with paper towels and replace the paper towels under the salmon with fresh, dry ones. Refrigerate the fish, uncovered, and cure for 3 days more. Turn them once a day, and change the paper towels each time you do so. When the salmon is ready, cut it into 4 equal pieces.

Preheat a grill to medium. Brush and oil the grate well. Grill the salmon until it browns and sizzles, about 3 minutes per side. Serve immediately with *daikon oroshi* and soy sauce.

Curing Fish

Japanese have cured fish for millennia, naturally preserving them to protect against famine and to capitalize on seasonal bounty, like the annual autumn salmon run up the Ishiraki River in the far north. But beyond its practical purposes, curing transforms the very nature of the fish, concentrating its flesh; developing rich umami compounds; and creating a more complex, flavorful food. The recipes that follow are a quartet of age-old traditional curing techniques for fish that taste incredible when grilled.

Miso-Cured Spanish Mackerel

The lightly fermented signature miso of Kyoto, *saikyo* miso, has a flavor that is delicately sweet rather than powerfully savory. Salting the mackerel overnight releases its water, giving the flesh room to absorb the miso. While the Spanish mackerel cures, the miso's bacteria cultures essentially pickle the fish and at the same time infuse it with its singular subtle flavors. Laying aluminum foil under the delicate fish prevents it from sticking and breaking apart. You can also use this method with pompano, yellowtail, and mahi mahi.

Serves 4

4 Spanish mackerel fillets (1½ to 2 pounds)

Salt

⅔ cup saikyo miso (page 7)

2 tablespoons mirin

Season the fillets with salt all over. Cover with plastic wrap and refrigerate for 12 hours, or overnight. Wipe off moisture that accumulates on the surface of the fish with paper towels.

Mix together the miso and mirin in a bowl. Choose a glass baking dish or plastic container large enough to lay the fillets flat. (If they all don't fit in one row, you can pack the fish in layers, one over the other.) With a rubber spatula, smear a thick coat of miso mixture on the bottom of the vessel. Lay the fillets on top of the mixture. With a rubber spatula or your fingers, coat the top of the Spanish mackerel with more of the mixture until it's entirely encased. If you need to add another layer of fillets, place them on top and coat them thoroughly with more miso. Cover or wrap tightly with plastic wrap. Cure the fish in the refrigerator for 3 days. Wipe off as much miso as possible from the surface of the fish with paper towels.

Preheat a grill to medium-hot. Brush the cooking grate clean and oil it well. Place a sheet of aluminum foil on the grill and lay the Spanish mackerel fillets on top (so they don't burn). Grill for about 3 minutes per side, carefully turning the fillets with two fish spatulas so they don't break apart. Serve immediately.

Sakekasu-Cured Black Cod

Sakekasu is the fermented rice mash, or lees, left over from producing sake once the liquid—sake—is pressed out of it. Although the sake is gone, *sakekasu* retains an intense sake flavor, alcohol, and a rich bacteria culture. Like miso, it's also used to preserve and transform the flavor of fish through curing. We salt the fish overnight to remove water molecules so the *sakekasu* can be absorbed in the flesh. You can find *sakekasu* in the freezer section of Japanese markets.

Serves 4

4 (1-inch-thick) black cod fillets, about 2 pounds

Salt

½ pound sakekasu (about 1 cup, if using the creamy style), at room temperature

¼ cup mirin

2 tablespoons soy sauce

Season the black cod fillets with salt all over. Cover with plastic wrap and refrigerate for 12 hours, or overnight. Wipe off moisture that accumulates on the surface of the fish with paper towels.

Add the *sakekasu*, mirin, and soy sauce to the jar of a blender. Pulse until it becomes a smooth paste, about 1 minute. Choose a glass baking dish or plastic container large enough to lay the fillets flat. With a rubber spatula, smear a thick coat of *sakekasu* mixture on the bottom of the vessel. Lay the fillets on top of the mixture. With a rubber spatula or your fingers, coat the top of the fish with more of the mixture until it's entirely encased. If you need to add another layer of fillets, place them on top and coat them thoroughly with more *sakekasu* mixture. Cover or wrap tightly with plastic wrap. Cure the fish in the refrigerator for 3 days. Wipe off as much *sakekasu* mixture as possible from the surface of the fish with paper towels.

Preheat a grill to medium-hot. Brush the cooking grate clean and oil it well. Place a sheet of aluminum foil on the grill and lay the black cod fillets on top (so they don't burn—black cod is very oily). Grill for about 5 minutes per side, carefully turning the fillets with two fish spatulas so they don't break apart. The skin may stick to the foil; that's okay. Serve immediately.

Bronzini Himono

With this age-old technique, you "half-dry" fish, curing it to naturally preserve and enhance its flavor, but not drying it completely so the fish still retains its character. Across Japan in winter, you can still see fish hanging to dry outside of rural homes. Sunshine firms up the surface of the fish and browns it slightly. Instead of hanging outside, though, we keep it in the refrigerator overnight to dehydrate and cure further. *Himono*-style fish is very popular in Japan, and not just in the countryside. *Izakayas* (eating pubs) serve *hokke*, a type of mackerel, this way, too. If you'd like, you can enjoy this fish with soy sauce and *daikon oroshi* (page 73). Half-dried fish also freezes well, so why not double the recipe and save some for later? Freeze for up to one month. Besides bronzini, try the *himono* technique with sea bass, snapper, porgy, trout, and sole.

Serves 4

3 tablespoons salt

4 cups water

4 bronzini (about 3 pounds), butterflied (ask your fish market to do this)

Put the salt and the 4 cups water in a large bowl and stir until the salt has dissolved. Add the bronzini and soak for 30 minutes to brine the fish. Dry the fish with paper towels. Place a wire rack on a tray large enough to hold the 4 fish flat. Dry the fish in direct sunshine for 1 hour on each side to cure it, firm up its texture, and concentrate its flavor. The bronzini will brown a little under the sun; that's okay. Place the fish in the refrigerator, uncovered, for 12 hours, or overnight, to cure it further.

Preheat a grill to hot. Grill the bronzini about 3 minutes. Start with the skin side down and gently turn the fish every minute until it browns. Serve immediately.

MEAT

EATING MEAT IS a relatively recent development in Japan, where butchering four-legged creatures was banned for about a thousand years, until the country opened to the West in the mid-nineteenth century. At that time, eating meat, loads of it, was the American version of health food (some things haven't changed), and the American and European visitors got the Japanese eating meat again (for more on this story, see "Meat in Japanese Cooking," page 2). But the way Japanese expressed their appreciation for meat is distinctly different from Western styles. Instead of as a thick steak, in Japan meat is usually enjoyed thinly sliced, a nod to the Japanese chopstick culture and perhaps, too, a more natural fit for a cuisine where delicate slices of raw fish are so fundamental. And instead of dense dry-aged beef, Japanese prize the rich, tender flesh of wagyu (see "Wagyu," page 102), thin, delicate slices of meat that are typically grilled quickly on *shichirin* or *konro* grills fueled by traditional binchotan charcoal (see "Binchotan," page 12). In this chapter we pay homage to classic Japanese beef and pork grilling methods, as well as embrace the way we eat meat here in America—but give our American-style steaks, chops, and loins a distinctly Japanese sensibility. Because, as people in Japan already know, nothing boosts the taste of grilled meat like soy sauce, miso, mirin, sake, and other traditional seasonings. We love grilling American-style with Japanese flavors, and when you taste the mouthwatering dishes and marinades in this chapter, we know you'll fall for these irresistible tastes, too.

Tempering

You are tempering meat when you let it come to room temperature before you grill. Why do it? Think about slapping a cold slab of meat straight out of the fridge onto the fire. By the time it warms enough to cook, and then cooks, you'll be left with a hunk of charcoal. Always temper your ingredients—all meat, chicken, and fish. "Room temperature," by the way, typically means anywhere from 68°F to 80°F. Use common sense. Tempering by a window with blazing hot sunshine pouring in is not a good idea. Letting meat sit on a counter in a cooler part of the kitchen—great. How long to temper? Thirty minutes for a thick steak, up to an hour for a whole chicken, or more or less, depending on the thickness of the food.

Resting

This happens after your meat is grilled. If you pull a gorgeous, perfectly grilled steak off the grill and cut into it immediately, the juices will pour out of it like rainwater from a flood pipe. Why? Searing the flesh concentrates the juices away from the edges and into the center. By resting, that is, letting cooked meat sit for 2, 3, 5, or 10 minutes away from heat (depending on the thickness of the cut), you're giving its internal juices time to redistribute back to every corner of the protein. Also, while resting, the meat continues to cook with its own residual heat (and will therefore stay warm). Resting ensures a moist, mouthwatering morsel in every bite. This goes for all meat (except for thin fillets), chicken, and some fish (depending on the thickness). We tell you how long to rest in the recipes.

Wagyu

Prized for its profound marbling, sublime beefy flavor, and melt-in-your-mouth tenderness, wagyu is the name for Japan's native breed of cattle, which yields the most expensive meat in the world. In the late nineteenth century, the Japanese emperor restored cattle herding to his country, lifting the centuries-old prohibition against cattle breeding. Farmers began raising beef cattle in isolated pockets, but because Japan is so mountainous and rugged, they had almost no room to range their herds. So they thought up inventive ways to raise cattle—including massaging them to counter muscle cramps from moving so little and feeding them beer and sake—which is how these cows developed the singular characteristics that make their meat so tasty and sought after. Wagyu evolved into distinct varieties named after the regions from which they hail; Kobe beef is the most well-known here. Today, ranchers in Australia and America are also breeding wagyu, crossed with hardy native breeds like Black Angus, so finding this beef is becoming easier.

Garlic–Soy Sauce Marinade

When Tadashi arrived in America twenty-five years ago (to surf in Southern California, but that's another story), he discovered American-style grilling with its charred, thick, juicy steaks in all their glory, something he never saw in Japan. He quickly fell in love with this fiery cooking and from that moment on, became, well, a grilling fanatic. But Tadashi also knew how much Japanese seasonings enhance the taste of grilled meat and fish. So he came up with this indispensable marinade to lavish an irresistible dose of savory, garlicky flavor to any red meat and dense-fleshed fish like tuna, salmon, mahi mahi, swordfish, and shark. Keep this go-to marinade handy in the fridge throughout the grilling season, just like Tadashi does.

Makes about 1 cup

1/2 cup soy sauce

8 cloves garlic, grated

1/4 cup olive oil

2 teaspoons freshly ground black pepper

Whisk together the soy sauce, garlic, olive oil, and black pepper in a small bowl. This marinade can keep in the refrigerator for up to 2 weeks. Just mix again before using it.

Gyu Dare Dipping Sauce and Marinade

Gyu dare (pronounced "guh-you dareh") means "beef sauce" in Japanese. Our version is an all-purpose dipping sauce and marinade that mingles together fundamental Japanese seasonings to add savoriness, acidity, body, and a hint of sweetness to meat. Use the *gyu dare* as a versatile flavor foundation onto which you can layer accents like wasabi, grated fresh ginger, grated garlic, grated horseradish, *shichimi togarashi*, *tobanjan*, *karashi* mustard, *ume* paste, or *yuzu kosho*. (Rule of thumb: add about 1 tablespoon of accent per 1 cup of *gyu dare*, or to taste.) You can also combine accents to create your own *gyu dare* variation and even add herbs like thyme, tarragon, basil, or shiso, or Tabasco sauce.

Makes about 2 cups

¾ cup soy sauce
½ cup sake
½ cup mirin
¼ cup rice vinegar

Add the soy sauce, sake, mirin, and rice vinegar to a saucepan and bring it to a boil over medium heat. Boil for 1 minute, remove from the heat, and let the liquid cool to room temperature. Before using, refrigerate for at least 12 hours, or overnight, to give the flavors time to mingle. *Gyu dare* can keep in the refrigerator for up to 1 month.

Thin-Sliced Tenderloin with Wasabi Gyu Dare

Called *gyu amiyaki*, this is the most popular way to enjoy grilled beef in Japan: thin-sliced, quickly charred over coals, and dipped into a tasty sauce. It's long been a picnic standard, with family and friends gathered around portable charcoal *shichirin* grills (page 11) and roasting the slices over the fire in leisurely rounds. We use delicate tenderloin here; richly marbled wagyu slices (see "Wagyu," page 102) work perfectly, too. You can also substitute *gyu dare* with ponzu (see "Ponzu," page 69) if you prefer a vinegary, citrusy accent.

Serves 4

1 cup Gyu Dare Dipping Sauce and Marinade (page 104)

1 tablespoon wasabi

1 1/2 pounds beef tenderloin, cut into 1/4-inch slices, about 8 to 12 pieces (ask your butcher to do this)

Salt

Freshly ground black pepper

Make the dipping sauce by whisking together the *gyu dare* and wasabi in a bowl. Divide between 4 small dipping bowls; set aside.

Lightly season the tenderloin slices with salt and pepper on one side only, so you don't overseason the meat.

Preheat a grill to hot. Brush the cooking grate clean and oil it well. Grill the tenderloin for about 1 minute per side, until it browns and sizzles. Serve immediately with the dipping sauce on the side.

Grilling in a Hurry?

Plan ahead! Keep plenty of Gyu Dare Dipping Sauce and Marinade (page 104), Garlic–Soy Sauce Marinade (page 103), and Yuzu Kosho Marinade (page 74) handy in the fridge (all last for weeks refrigerated). And the next time you buy a steak or pork chop and want to grill it—now—you'll be ready. Three speedy suggestions: Season a steak with salt and pepper, grill, and dip into *gyu dare*. Fast-marinate a steak in garlic–soy sauce marinade and grill. Or, fast-marinate pork in *yuzu kosho* marinade and grill.

Porterhouse
with Garlic–Soy Sauce Marinade

With a T-shaped bone that divides a cut of dense strip loin from a chunk of buttery tenderloin, the porterhouse is the iconic steak of American grilling. It's such a perfect steak that you don't want to do too much to it. Here we simply marinate it with the garlic–soy sauce marinade to give it a bit more oomph, but that's it. Also use this method to grill a T-bone steak, which is a smaller version of the porterhouse, or a beefy, marbled strip steak (also called shell or short loin). Adjust the grilling times to the size of the cut.

Serves 4

³/₄ cup Garlic–Soy Sauce Marinade (page 103)

2 (1¹/₂-inch-thick) porterhouse steaks, about 3¹/₂ pounds

Pour three-fourths of the marinade into a baking dish or rimmed sheet pan and reserve the rest. Lay the steaks in the marinade and flip them 4 times to generously coat all over. Marinate the steaks for 10 minutes.

Preheat a grill for a two-zone fire (medium and hot; see page 15). Grill the steaks for about 11 minutes for medium. With the grill covered, start on hot heat for 1 minute, then shift the steaks to medium heat. After about 4 minutes, juices will begin to appear on top of the meat. Flip the steaks and repeat the two-zone grilling on the other side. Once you turn the steaks, brush with the reserved marinade. Uncover the steak and grill for 1 more minute on hot heat to caramelize the marinade, flipping the steak 2 times and brushing with marinade after each turn. When the steaks are ready, they'll be browned, glossy, and juicy on the surface, and the bone will stick out a bit, as the meat around has shrunk. Test for doneness using the "The 'Nick-and-Peek' Method" (see page 111). Let the porterhouse rest for about 5 minutes. Slice the steaks against the grain and transfer to a platter. Pour the juices released during slicing over the meat and serve.

Sirloin Steak
with Karashi Mustard Gyu Dare

The sirloin, butchered from the hip section of the cow, is a more economical cut of steak with a good balance of tenderness and beefy flavor. Here we use both the garlic–soy sauce marinade and *karashi* mustard *gyu dare* to infuse the meat with bold flavors. You can also substitute the gyu dare with straight mustard by combining equal amounts of *karashi* mustard and Dijon mustard (*karashi* on its own is too strong) and dabbing it on the steak.

Serves 4

$^1/_2$ cup Garlic-Soy Sauce Marinade (page 103)

4 (1 inch) sirloin steaks, about 2 pounds

1 cup gyu dare (page 104)

1 tablespoon karashi mustard

Pour the marinade onto a baking dish or rimmed sheet pan. Lay the steaks in the marinade and flip them 4 times to generously coat all over.

Make the dipping sauce by whisking together the *gyu dare* and *karashi* mustard in a bowl. Divide between 4 small dipping bowls; set aside.

Preheat a grill to medium-hot. Grill the steaks, covered, for about 5 minutes for medium-rare this way: Turn the steaks after about 2 minutes, then turn a couple of more times during the last minute of grilling to give the steaks a nice charred finish. Test for doneness using "The 'Nick-and-Peek' Method" (see page 111). Let the steaks rest for 3 minutes and serve with the dipping sauce on the side.

Bone-In Rib-Eye with Wasabi Sour Cream

A bone-in rib-eye has the boomerang-shaped rib bone attached to the meat, which imparts incredible flavor and juiciness to the steak as it grills. Boneless rib-eye also works great with this method. Either cut, these steaks are laced with chunks of fat and nice marbling that give them a rich, full-on beefy flavor. Marinate with the garlic–soy sauce mixture to enhance this taste and finish with a dollop of wasabi-infused sour cream to offer kick and contrast.

Serves 4

½ cup sour cream

2 tablespoons wasabi

½ cup Garlic–Soy Sauce Marinade (page 103)

2 (1-inch-thick) rib-eye steaks, about 2 pounds

To make the wasabi sauce, mix the sour cream and wasabi in a bowl; set aside.

Pour the marinade into a baking dish or rimmed sheet pan. Lay the steaks in the marinade and flip them 4 times to generously coat all over. Marinate the steaks for 10 minutes.

Preheat a grill for a two-zone fire (medium and hot; see page 15). Grill the steaks, covered, about 8 minutes for medium-rare this way. Start on hot heat for 1 minute, then shift the steaks to medium heat. After about 3 minutes, juices will begin to appear on top of the steaks. Turn and repeat the two-zone grilling on the other side. When the steaks are ready, they'll be browned and juicy on the surface, and the bone will stick out a bit, as the meat around it has shrunk. Test for doneness using "The 'Nick-and-Peek' Method" (see page 111). Let the steaks rest for about 3 minutes. Slice the steaks against the grain and transfer to a platter. Pour the juices released during slicing over the meat, dollop with the wasabi sauce, and serve.

Filet Mignon with Ume Gyu Dare

Filet mignon is cut from the tenderloin, which, as the name implies, is the most tender meat on a cow. It's tender, but not particularly beefy, so we pair it with a tangy *ume*-infused *gyu dare* dipping sauce to give each bite more character.

Serves 4

4 (1¹/₂-inch-thick) filet mignon steaks, about 2 pounds

Salt

Freshly ground black pepper

1 cup Gyu Dare Dipping Sauce and Marinade (page 104)

1 tablespoon ume paste (page 7)

Season the steaks on all sides with salt and pepper.

Make the dipping sauce by whisking together the *gyu dare* and *ume* paste in a bowl. Divide between 4 small dipping bowls; set aside.

Preheat a grill for a two-zone fire (medium and hot; page 15). Clean and thoroughly oil the grate. Grill the steaks, covered, about 8 minutes for medium-rare. Start on hot heat for 1 minute, then shift the steaks to medium heat. After about 3 minutes, juices will begin to appear on top of the meat. Flip the steaks and repeat the two-zone grilling on the other side. When the steaks are ready, they'll be browned and juicy on the surface. Test for doneness using "The 'Nick-and-Peek' Method" (see below). Let the filet mignons rest for about 5 minutes. Serve with the dipping sauce on the side.

When Is It Done? The "Nick-and-Peek" Method

How do you know when your meat is done? A meat thermometer sounds great in theory, but good luck getting an accurate read on a fiery grill. And internal temperature guidelines can be confusing; your steak could end up like shoe leather. So what to do? Nick and peek. After following the grill temperature level and timing in our recipes, pull the meat off the grill and cut a small incision into it. Check the color inside. Steaks, lamb, and ribs cooked medium-rare will look deep pink; cooked pork will be white and juicy, with no pink; chicken will be white, and the juices will run clear.

"Tokyo Broil" Flank Steak

This is the Japanese version of that summertime grilling classic—the London broil. We use flank steak for this recipe, but shoulder steak, top round, and bottom round also work well. All of these are lean cuts of meat, so you have to marinate them overnight to tenderize and infuse flavors into the beef.

Serves 4

2 pounds (1¹/₂-inch-thick) flank steak

³/₄ cup Gyu Dare Dipping Sauce and Marinade (page 104)

4 cloves garlic, finely grated

1 tablespoon grated fresh ginger

2 teaspoons shichimi togarashi (page 7)

1 tablespoon sesame oil

¹/₂ teaspoon salt

Make 3 or 4 slashing cuts lengthwise across the grain of the steak, about ¹/₂ inch deep, so the marinade can better penetrate the meat.

To make the marinade, mix together the *gyu dare*, garlic, ginger, *shichimi togarashi*, sesame oil, and salt in a bowl. Pour the marinade into a baking dish or rimmed sheet pan. Lay the steak in the marinade and flip it 4 times to generously coat all over. Cover the meat with plastic wrap and refrigerate for 12 hours, or overnight.

Preheat a grill to medium. Grill the steak, covered, about 16 minutes to medium-rare, flipping it about every 4 minutes. When the steak is ready, it will be browned and glossy. Test for doneness using "The 'Nick-and-Peek' Method" (see page 111). Let the steak rest for about 5 minutes. Slice the steak against the grain and transfer to a platter. Pour the juices released during slicing over the meat and serve.

Skirt Steak with Red Miso

This rich, fatty cut from the underside of the cow comes in a long, thin, flat strip. It's one of our favorites—skirt steak grills quickly and is incredibly juicy and flavorful. Here we pair it with a spicy, garlicky miso marinade that stands up to the steak's bold flavors. Thick miso needs time to penetrate the meat, so you have to marinate longer than with soy sauce–based marinades.

Serves 4

5 cloves garlic, finely grated

6 tablespoons red miso (page 6)

2 tablespoons mirin

2 tablespoons sake

1 tablespoon tobanjan (page 7)

2 tablespoons sugar

2 pounds skirt steak, extra fat trimmed off, cut into 4 equal pieces

To make the marinade, mix together the garlic, red miso, mirin, sake, *tobanjan*, and sugar in a bowl. Pour the marinade into a baking dish or rimmed sheet pan. Lay the skirt steak in the marinade and flip it 4 times to generously coat all over. Marinate the steak for 1 hour at room temperature, turning once.

Preheat a grill to medium-hot. Grill the skirt steak about 3 minutes per side, to medium-rare. The steak might stick to the grill because of the miso, so ease it off carefully. (A bit of charred miso adds wonderful flavor and fragrance.) Test for doneness using "The 'Nick-and-Peek' Method" (see page 111). Let the skirt steak rest for 2 minutes and serve.

VARIATION The red miso marinade works perfectly with hanger steak, sirloin, or flat-iron steak (also called top blade). Allow the meat to marinate for 1 hour and grill.

The Power of Miso

We love marinating beef with miso because the miso both tenderizes the meat and adds incredible flavor. With the skirt steak recipe (above) and Hatcho Miso-Marinated Hanger Steak (page 114), we call for marinating the steaks for one hour at room temperature. But if you've got the time and the will, try marinating for one, two, even three days in the refrigerator. The results will amaze you. The longer the meat marinades in the miso, the more it turns buttery tender and delicious—the result of miso's bacteria and enzymes breaking down and penetrating the meat at a leisurely pace.

Hatcho-Miso–Marinated Hanger Steak

Known as "the butcher's tenderloin" because it's so flavorful butchers once saved it for themselves, hanger steak is a muscle attached to the diaphragm, and there's only one of these gems per cow. These steaks are rich, juicy, and incredibly beefy. Here we pair hanger with dense, intense *Hatcho* miso, spiked with other classic Japanese flavorings, to offer a bold, mouthwatering counterpoint to this cut.

Serves 4

2 pounds hanger steak, sliced in half horizontally to about 1/2 inch thick (ask your butcher to do this)

1/4 cup Hatcho miso (page 7)

5 cloves garlic, finely grated

2 tablespoons mirin

3 tablespoons sake

2 tablespoons vinegar

2 tablespoons chopped scallions (white and green parts), plus 2 tablespoons thinly sliced scallions

2 tablespoons sesame oil

1 tablespoon soy sauce

2 teaspoons freshly ground black pepper

With a meat pounder, mallet, or the side of a heavy knife or cleaver, pound the steak 6 times to flatten and condense the meat; reserve.

Add the *Hatcho* miso, garlic, mirin, sake, vinegar, the 2 tablespoons chopped scallions, sesame oil, soy sauce, and black pepper to a jar of a blender. Cover and pulse until the ingredients are combined into a smooth paste, about 1 minute. Pour the marinade into a baking dish or rimmed sheet pan. Lay the hanger steak in the marinade and flip it 4 times to generously coat all over. Marinate the steak for 1 hour at room temperature, turning once.

Preheat a grill to medium-hot. Grill the hanger steak about 3 minutes per side to medium-rare. The steak might stick to the grill because of the miso, so ease it off carefully. (A bit of charred miso adds wonderful flavor and fragrance.) Test for doneness using "The 'Nick-and-Peek' Method" (see page 111). Let the hanger steak rest for 2 minutes. Sprinkle the 2 tablespoons sliced scallions on top and serve.

VARIATIONS If you prefer, you can grill the whole hanger steak without slicing it in half horizontally. Grill the steak, covered, about 12 minutes, turning twice, to medium-rare.

The *Hatcho* miso marinade works perfectly with skirt steak, sirloin, or flat-iron steak (also called top blade). Allow the meat to marinate for 1 hour and grill.

Grilled Wagyu with Ponzu

Because wagyu (see "Wagyu," page 102) is so incredibly marbled and rich, you don't want to bite into a thick hunk of it. The best way to eat it is thinly sliced and quickly grilled, as we do here, which lets you enjoy all the fatty goodness and pillowy tenderness of wagyu, without being overwhelmed by it. The acidic ponzu is a classic counterpoint to grilled wagyu. Or you can just stick to the salt and pepper for seasoning and savor a hit of straight-up wagyu beefiness.

Serves 4

4 (1/4-inch-thick) wagyu rib-eye steaks, about 1 pound

Salt

Freshly ground black pepper

1 cup Ponzu (page 69)

1 tablespoon yuzu kosho (page 7)

1/2 cup Daikon Oroshi, (page 73)

Lightly season the wagyu with salt and pepper on one side only (so not to overseason this thin meat). If you're using ponzu straight out of the refrigerator, let it come to room temperature; divide between 4 small bowls and set aside.

Preheat a grill to hot. Brush and oil the grate. Grill the wagyu until the meat is browned and sizzling, about 1 1/2 minutes per side and cooked to medium-rare. Don't worry if you have flare ups, since this is fast grilling. Let the wagyu rest for 2 minutes and serve. To eat, add the *yuzu kosho* and *daikon oroshi* to the ponzu and dip in slices of the wagyu.

Scallion Beef

Called *gyu negi maki*, this is a favorite dish at *izakayas* (eating pubs) across Japan. Thin slices of beef are wrapped around scallions (or Japanese *negi*) and basted with a glossy, savory marinade while grilling. The sharpness of the scallions cuts the richness of the marinated beef. You can find thin-sliced beef at Asian markets, Japanese markets (look for sukiyaki beef), or Korean markets (look for bulgogi beef). Wagyu (see "Wagyu," page 102) is also terrific with this dish.

Serves 4

1/4 cup soy sauce

1 tablespoon mirin

1 tablespoon sake

1/2 teaspoon freshly ground black pepper

1 pound rib-eye or sirloin, sliced horizontally paper thin (ask your butcher to do this)

12 scallions, both ends trimmed, so each is about 6 inches long

12 toothpicks

Mix together the soy sauce, mirin, sake, and black pepper in a bowl to make the marinade; set aside.

Divide the beef into 4 equal portions. Arrange 1 portion into an approximately 6-inch-wide "sheet," overlapping the slices. Place 3 of the scallions lengthwise along one side of the beef: 2 scallions with the white parts in one direction, 1 scallion with the white part in the other direction. Roll the beef around the scallions. Secure the roll with 3 evenly spaced toothpicks. Repeat with the remaining portions of beef and scallions to make 4 rolls.

Preheat a grill to hot. Brush and oil the grate well. Grill the rolls for about 6 minutes total, turning every 20 to 30 seconds. If you have a flare-up, shift the rolls to another part of the grate or use a spray bottle. After about 3 minutes, brush on the marinade. Keep grilling and turning the rolls for 3 more minutes, brushing them with more marinade after every turn. When they're done, the rolls will be browned, glossy, and glazed. Transfer the rolls to a cutting board and let them rest for 1 minute. Remove the toothpicks, cut each roll in 4 equal parts, and serve.

Two-Minute Steak with Shiso Butter

With this quick steak preparation, you can keep both the pounded steaks and compound butter handy in the freezer, to defrost and grill in no time. The shiso butter bestows richness and flavor to the thin steak, which also benefits from the garlic–soy sauce marinade. Note that the flavored butter must chill at least 1 hour before using.

Serves 4

4 ounces unsalted butter (1 stick), at room temperature

2 bunches shiso leaves (about 20 leaves), very thinly sliced

1/4 teaspoon salt

2 (1/2-inch-thick) sirloin steaks, about 1 pound, sliced in half horizontally to make 4 pieces (ask your butcher to do this)

1/2 cup Garlic-Soy Sauce Marinade (page 103)

To make the shiso butter, add the butter, shiso leaves, and the 1/4 teaspoon salt to the bowl of a food processor. Pulse just until the shiso incorporates with the butter, about 30 seconds.

When the butter is ready, lay a 12-inch-long piece of plastic wrap on a work surface. Place the shiso butter on the plastic wrap, creating a 4-inch-long mound parallel to the edge of the work surface closest to you. Roll up the plastic wrap as tightly as you can, to shape the butter into a fat sausage about 1 1/2 inches in diameter. To secure the ends, grasp the ends of the plastic wrap, lift the butter, and spin it over itself several times, to tighten as much as possible. Place the butter in the refrigerator until it hardens, at least 1 hour.

Wrap each of the 4 pieces of steak in plastic wrap. Using a meat pounder, mallet, or the side of a heavy knife or cleaver, pound the steaks to about 1/4 inch thick. Make sure to pound both sides of the meat.

Pour the marinade onto a baking dish or rimmed sheet pan. Lay the meat in the marinade and flip the pieces 4 times to generously coat both sides of the meat.

Preheat a grill to hot. Grill the steaks for about 2 minutes, turning once, until the meat is browned. Top the steaks with 1/4-inch-thick slices of shiso butter and serve.

VARIATION Use the shiso butter to top all kinds of grilled steak and grilled pork, veal, chicken breast, and salmon. Shiso butter stores well, tightly wrapped, in the freezer.

Japanese Burgers with Wasabi Ketchup

Think of this burger as a "burger steak"—a totally different eating experience than the good ol' American version. This burger is a mixture of ground beef, pork, and milk-soaked panko breadcrumbs (flaky Japanese-style crumbs), which makes it incredibly juicy and moist. You don't eat it with a bun. Instead, serve it on a plate like a steak with rice on the side or in the center of a sliced *yaki onigiri* (page 155). You can substitute the wasabi in the ketchup recipe with yuzu kosho, *karashi* mustard, or Tabasco (but use 1/2 to 1 teaspoon of each). Finally, these burgers make excellent sliders, so slap together a bunch of tiny patties for appetizers and tuck them into similarly sized *yaki onigiri*.

Serves 4

WASABI KETCHUP

1/2 cup ketchup

2 tablespoons soy sauce

1 tablespoon wasabi

JAPANESE BURGERS

1/2 cup panko breadcrumbs (or regular dried breadcrumbs)

1/4 cup whole milk

1/2 pound ground sirloin beef

1/2 pound ground pork

1/4 teaspoon freshly ground black pepper

1/4 cup finely chopped white onion

1/2 tablespoon soy sauce

1/2 teaspoon salt

Sesame oil, for coating hands

To make the wasabi ketchup, whisk together the ketchup, soy sauce, and wasabi in a bowl; set aside.

To make the burgers, mix together the breadcrumbs and milk in a bowl and let sit until the breadcrumbs absorb all the milk, about 5 minutes. When the breadcrumbs are ready, mix them together with the ground beef, ground pork, black pepper, onion, soy sauce, and salt in a large bowl. Knead the meat until it becomes sticky and binds together; divide the mixture into 4 equal parts. Lightly dab your hands with sesame oil. Using your palms, roll each part of the meat into a ball, then pat the ball flat, shifting it from hand to hand, to form a 1/2-inch-thick patty (patting like this compresses the meat and removes air pockets). Press down to make an indentation in the center of the patty (which prevents the patty from puffing up into a ball while it grills). Place the completed patties on a sheet of aluminum foil.

(continued)

Preheat a grill to medium. Grill the burgers until they're nicely browned, about 10 minutes, flipping twice. These burgers have to cook through completely because of the pork; you'll see no pink in the middle, but they'll still be incredibly juicy and tasty. Let the burgers rest for 2 minutes. Spoon the wasabi ketchup on top and serve.

Karashi Mustard Short Ribs

These flavorful, fatty chunks of short ribs work great on the grill. The trick is to grill them bone side down for most of the time; the bone stops the rest of the meat from burning up, giving the thick, juicy cut time to leisurely cook through. The grill's cover also comes in handy here, preventing flare-ups as fat drips, drips, drips down from the ribs. The sharp *karashi* mustard cuts through all this fabulous fattiness and adds an appealing kick.

Serves 4

2 pounds short ribs, cut into 4 pieces (each about 3 inches long and 2 inches thick; ask your butcher to do this)

1 teaspoon salt, plus more for seasoning the meat

1 tablespoon freshly ground black pepper, plus more for seasoning the meat

2 tablespoons karashi mustard

2 tablespoons balsamic vinegar

¼ cup soy sauce

1 tablespoon sugar

Generously season the short ribs with salt and freshly ground pepper all over. Whisk together the mustard, balsamic vinegar, soy sauce, sugar, the 1 tablespoon pepper, and the 1 teaspoon salt in a bowl to make the marinade; set aside.

Preheat a grill to medium. Grill the short ribs, covered, this way: Start with the bone side up, grilling for about 5 minutes. Flip the short ribs, so the bone side is now down (the bone will prevent the meat from burning), and brush the marinade on top. Grill about 15 more minutes, brushing with more marinade on top 3 more times. When the short ribs are ready, they'll be richly browned and glossy. Test for doneness using "The 'Nick-and-Peek' Method" (see page 111). Let the short ribs rest for 5 minutes and serve.

"Kalbi"-Style Short Ribs

These are the same short ribs as in the previous recipe, but cut Korean-style into 1/4-inch-thick strips. Marinating and grilling this special cut make a signature Korean dish that is also enormously popular in Japan. You can find this cut of short ribs at Korean and Japanese food markets. Once you've marinated the ribs, you can refrigerate them for up to 3 days in case you want to grill another batch (and once you taste them, that's exactly what you'll want to do). By the way, "kalbi"-style ribs are fantastic with a bowl of rice.

Serves 4

4 cloves garlic

1/2 teaspoon salt

1 tablespoon sugar

2 tablespoons chopped scallions (white and green parts)

1 tablespoon sesame seed

1 tablespoon sesame oil

1/4 cup plus 2 tablespoons soy sauce

1 tablespoon mirin

1 tablespoon sake

1 teaspoon vinegar

1 teaspoon tobanjan (page 7)

2 pounds short ribs, cut crosswise into 1/4-inch-thick slices (ask your butcher to do this)

To make the marinade, add all the ingredients except for the short ribs into the jar of a blender. Pulse until you have a smooth mixture, about 1 minute (it's okay to see flecks of scallion and sesame seed). Pour the marinade into a baking dish or rimmed sheet pan. Lay the short ribs in the marinade and flip them 4 times to generously coat all over. Marinate the ribs for 15 minutes at room temperature.

Preheat a grill to hot. Brush and oil the grate. Grill the short ribs until the meat is browned and sizzling, about 2 minutes per side to medium-rare. Don't worry if you have flare-ups, since this is fast grilling. Serve immediately.

Veal Cutlets with Ponzu Butter

Here's another fast-grilling preparation. The veal cutlets are tender and juicy, and the ponzu butter infuses them with citrus, heat, and, of course, richness. The flavored butter must sit in the refrigerator at least 1 hour before serving. Use it with pork chops, steak, chicken breasts, and salmon. It also freezes well.

Serves 4

6 ounces unsalted butter (1½ sticks), at room temperature

½ cup Ponzu (page 69)

½ teaspoon yuzu kosho (page 7)

2 tablespoons finely chopped fresh chives (or the green parts of scallions)

4 veal cutlets (about 1½ pounds)

Salt

Freshly ground black pepper

To make the ponzu butter, add the butter, *ponzu, yuzu kosho*, and chives to the work bowl of a food processor. Pulse just until the ponzu and butter blend and all the ingredients bind together, about 30 seconds. You want no liquid left, but be careful not to overprocess, or the butter will begin to separate.

When the butter is ready, lay a 12-inch-long piece of plastic wrap on a work surface. Scoop out the *ponzu* butter and place it on the plastic wrap, creating a 4-inch-long mound parallel to the edge of the work surface closest to you. Roll up the plastic wrap as tightly as you can to shape the butter into a fat sausage about 1½ inches in diameter. To secure the ends, grasp the ends of the plastic wrap, lift the butter, and spin it over itself several times to tighten as much as possible. Tuck the ends of the plastic wrap under the butter so they don't unravel and place the butter in the refrigerator until it hardens, at least 1 hour.

Wrap each piece of veal in plastic wrap. Using a meat pounder, mallet, or the side of a heavy knife or cleaver, pound the veal to about ¼ inch thick. Make sure to pound both sides of the meat. Season the veal with salt and black pepper all over.

Preheat a grill to medium-hot. Grill the veal for about 2 minutes, turning once. Top each cutlet with a ½-inch-thick slice of ponzu butter and serve immediately.

Veal Chops with Shiitake Dashi

Shiitake dashi, or stock derived from dried shiitake, is a classic Japanese ingredient. When the naturally preserved fungi are reconstituted, they create intensely mushroomy, concentrated, and umami-rich flavor. The fragrant shiitake dashi perfectly complements the tender grilled veal chops.

Serves 4

SHIITAKE DASHI

1/2-ounce whole dried shiitake mushrooms (6 to 12 pieces)

2 cups water

1/2 cup sake

1/4 cup soy sauce

2 tablespoons mirin

1 tablespoon cornstarch

1 tablespoon water

VEAL CHOPS

4 veal chops (about 4 pounds)

Salt

Freshly ground black pepper

To prepare the shiitake dashi, add the shiitake and the 2 cups water to a saucepan and let the mushrooms soak at room temperature 12 hours, or overnight. Drain the shiitake (leave the soaking water in the saucepan) and transfer them to a cutting board. Trim off and discard the stems and thinly slice the mushrooms. Return the mushrooms to the liquid in the saucepan. Add the sake, soy sauce, and mirin to the saucepan and bring it to a boil over medium heat. Decrease the heat so the liquid simmers; cook until the liquid reduces by two-thirds, about 30 minutes. Skim off any scum that appears on the surface. While the dashi simmers, combine the cornstarch and water in a small bowl and set aside. When the dashi has reduced, remove the saucepan from heat. Add the cornstarch mixture and stir until the dashi thickens. Let the dashi come to room temperature.

To prepare the veal, season the chops all over with salt and black pepper.

Preheat a grill to medium-hot. Grill the chops for about 5 minutes per side for medium-rare. When the chops are done, the bone will stick out, as the meat around it has shrunk, and the veal will be a rich caramel color. Test for doneness using "The 'Nick-and-Peek' Method" (see page 111). Let the chops rest for about 3 minutes. Drizzle the shiitake dashi over the veal chops and serve.

VARIATION Drizzle the dashi over steak, pork chops, and burgers. It keeps refrigerated for 3 weeks and freezes well.

Pork Chops with Yuzu-Miso Marinade

With these pork chops, you marinate the meat in miso overnight for two reasons: First, it takes time for the pork to absorb the miso flavor. Second, it gives the active bacteria cultures in miso time to tenderize the meat. The result is tender, lip-smacking chops with a pleasing touch of heat from the *yuzu kosho*.

Serves 4

¼ cup red miso (page 6)

1 tablespoon sake

1 tablespoon mirin

2 teaspoons red yuzu kosho (page 7)

¼ cup finely chopped scallions (white and green parts)

1 tablespoon plus 1 teaspoon sesame oil

4 bone-in pork chops (about 1½ pounds)

Mix together the miso, sake, mirin, *yuzu kosho*, scallions, and sesame oil in a bowl to make the marinade. Pour three-fourths of the marinade into a baking dish or rimmed sheet pan and reserve the rest. Lay the pork chops in the marinade and flip them 4 times to generously coat all over. Marinate the pork chops for 12 hours, or overnight, in the refrigerator.

Preheat a grill to a two-zone fire (medium and hot; see page 15). Grill the pork chops for about 10 minutes this way: Start on hot heat for about 1 minute, then shift the chops to medium heat. After about 4 minutes, flip the chops and repeat the two-zone grilling on the other side. When the pork is ready, it'll be glossy and juicy on the outside. Test for doneness using "The 'Nick-and-Peek' Method" (see page 111). Let the pork chops rest for about 2 minutes and serve.

Ginger Boneless Pork Shoulder

In Japan, this pork preparation, called *ton shoga yaki*, is typically sliced first to make it faster to grill. (The thinly sliced, marinated pork can also be stir-fried, instead of grilled.) If you can't find pork shoulder steaks, substitute ¹/₂-inch-thick slices of pork loin.

Serves 4

4 pork shoulder steaks (¹/₂ inch thick), about 1 pound

¹/₄ cup soy sauce

2 tablespoons olive oil

1 tablespoon grated fresh ginger

1 tablespoon sake

1 tablespoon mirin

Using a meat pounder, mallet, or the side of a heavy knife or cleaver, pound the pork 6 times to tenderize and condense the meat.

Mix together the soy sauce, olive oil, ginger, sake, and mirin in a bowl to make the marinade. Pour three-fourths of the marinade into a baking dish or rimmed sheet pan and reserve the rest. Lay the pork shoulder in the marinade and flip the meat 4 times to generously coat all over. Marinate the pork for 15 minutes, turning once.

Preheat a grill to a two-zone fire (medium and hot; see page 15). Grill the pork for about 9 minutes this way: Start on hot heat for about 1 minute, then shift the pork to medium heat. After about 3 minutes, flip the steaks and repeat the two-zone grilling on the other side. Once you turn the pork, brush with the reserved marinade..Grill for 1 more minute on hot heat to caramelize the marinade, flipping the pork 2 times and brushing with marinade after each turn. When the pork is ready, it'll be glossy and juicy on the outside. Test for doneness using "The 'Nick-and-Peek' Method" (see page 111). Let the pork rest for about 3 minutes and serve.

Chashu Pork

This Chinese style of grilling pork has been happily adopted in Japan, especially at ramen joints, where a slice of *chashu* is a standard topping for a steaming bowl of noodles. Ramen or not, slow-grilled *chashu* tastes incredible, especially served with a bowl of rice on the side. You can also chop it into small cubes and use it to make fried rice. If you can't find boneless pork shoulder, you can substitute pork loin. Make sure to eat *chashu* at room temperature, the way it's traditionally enjoyed.

Serves 4

½ cup soy sauce

¼ cup sake

2 tablespoons mirin

1 tablespoon packed brown sugar

4 thick slices unpeeled fresh ginger (about ½ ounce)

2 cloves garlic, crushed

2 small scallions (white and green parts), coarsely chopped

1½ pounds pork shoulder, boned and tied up with butcher's string (ask your butcher to do this for you)

To make the marinade, whisk together the soy sauce, sake, mirin, and sugar in a bowl until the sugar has dissolved. Add the ginger, garlic, and scallions. Pour three-fourths of the marinade into a baking dish or rimmed sheet pan and reserve the rest. Lay the pork in the marinade and flip it 4 times to generously coat all over. Cover and marinate the pork in the refrigerator for 2 hours, flipping the meat every 30 minutes.

Set up a grill for indirect heat (medium-low heat; see page 15). Grill the pork, covered, on the indirect side this way: Grill for about 10 minutes. Flip the pork and brush with the reserved marinade. Grill the meat for about 35 more minutes. Brush on more marinade about every 5 minutes. The pork will become browned and glossy when it's ready. Allow the pork to come to room temperature, cut into ¼-inch-thick slices, and serve.

Garlic-Miso Dipping Sauce

This dipping sauce pairs wonderfully with chicken, pork, or steak. Chopping the garlic (instead of grating) and mixing the sauce by hand help the sauce retain the characteristics of its individual ingredients, giving it a more complex flavor.

Makes about ³/₄ cup

2 cloves garlic, finely chopped

¹/₄ cup red miso (page 6)

¹/₄ cup thinly sliced scallions (white and green parts)

2 tablespoons sake

2 tablespoons sesame oil

2 tablespoons rice vinegar

1 teaspoon tobanjan (page 7)

Whisk together the garlic, miso, scallions, sake, sesame oil, vinegar, and *tobanjan* in a bowl. Do this by hand and not in a blender; you don't want to pulverize the garlic and scallions. This dipping sauce can keep in the refrigerator for 2 weeks. Mix well again before using.

Crispy Pork Belly
with Garlic-Miso Dipping Sauce

Because pork belly is so rich, marinades won't work with it—the marinade will drip off along with the pork fat while grilling. Instead, just salt and grill, which renders a lot of fat and turns the pork belly nice and crispy. Dipping it into the garlic-miso sauce adds a flavorful kick.

Serves 4

1¼ pounds pork belly (about 4 inches long), cut into ¼-inch slices

Salt

¾ cup Garlic-Miso Dipping Sauce (page 128), divided between 4 small dipping bowls

Lightly season the pork belly slices with salt all over.

Preheat a grill to medium. Grill the pork belly slices for about 5 minutes, flipping them about every 1 minute (frequent turning prevents the slices from curling and makes them evenly crisp). If you have flare-ups with this fatty cut, shift the slices or spray the flames with a water mister. Be careful not to burn the meat. Depending on the size of your grill, you may want to cook the pork belly in batches to leave enough room to shift the slices. Serve the pork belly immediately and eat with the dipping sauce.

Japanese-Style Barbecued Baby Back Ribs

This is a Japanese version of the grilling classic from the American South, which we promise will be just as bone-sucking good as the ribs you'll find in a Memphis pit barbecue. Instead of the traditional slow and low (temperature) method for ribs, with this recipe you braise the ribs until they're tender, then grill. This way, you'll get both fall-off-the-bone tenderness and nice caramelization and char—in other words, rib nirvana. Save the braising liquid; it cooks down into a phenomenal barbecue sauce. Besides using it with the ribs, you can also slather it over burgers, steaks, or pork chops.

Serves 4

2 racks baby back ribs (about 5 to 6 pounds)

6 cups water

1 whole unpeeled bulb garlic, halved horizontally across the mid-section

1 medium Spanish onion, coarsely chopped

1 medium carrot, coarsely chopped

1/2 cup tomato puree

1 cup sake

2 tablespoons rice vinegar

1/4 cup soy sauce

3 tablespoons sugar

2 tablespoons red miso (page 6)

1 tablespoon tobanjan (page 7)

1 teaspoon whole black peppercorns

1 tablespoon sesame seed, for accent

Cut each rack of baby back ribs in half, which will yield 4 portions of 5 to 6 ribs each. To a large stockpot, add the ribs, the 6 cups water, garlic, onion, carrot, tomato puree, sake, rice vinegar, soy sauce, sugar, miso, *tobanjan*, and peppercorns and bring to a boil over high heat. Decrease the heat so the liquid gently simmers. Remove any scum or oil that floats to the surface. Cover the pot and cook until the ribs become tender, about 1 hour.

Remove the ribs from the pot and set aside, reserving the cooking liquid. To make the marinade, bring the cooking liquid to a boil over high heat and boil until it reduces by half and becomes syrupy. Remove from the heat and allow the liquid to come to room temperature. Transfer the liquid to the jar of a blender, cover, and pulse until smooth, about 1 minute. Pass the liquid through a fine-meshed strainer suspended over a large bowl and discard any solids caught in the strainer. Set the marinade aside.

Preheat a grill to hot. Grill the ribs for about 4 minutes, flipping once. When the ribs are browned and sizzling, brush the marinade on top. Grill for about 2 more minutes, flipping 2 or 3 times, and brushing on more marinade after each turn. Let the ribs rest for 2 minutes. Accent with sesame seed and serve.

Pork Spare Ribs
with Miso-Sansho Marinade

Spare ribs are the big-boned, fatty ribs from the underside of a pig. Here we give these guys a Japanese touch. As they grill, the miso toasts and caramelizes and combines with the *sansho* to release an unbelievable aroma that we guarantee will make you ravenous (it made us ravenous, and then some). The taste of toasted miso is as appealing as its smell.

Serves 4

¼ cup red miso (page 6)

1 tablespoon sesame oil

2 tablespoons sake

3 tablespoons mirin

1 tablespoon sansho
(page 7)

12 pork spare ribs
(3 to 4 pounds), cut into
individual ribs

To make the marinade, mix together the miso, sesame oil, sake, mirin, and *sansho* in a bowl. Pour three-fourths of the marinade into a baking dish or rimmed sheet pan and reserve the rest. Lay the spare ribs in the marinade and flip them 4 times to generously coat all over. Marinate the spare ribs for 1 hour at room temperature.

Preheat a grill to medium. Grill the ribs, covered, this way: Start by grilling the ribs, bone side down, for about 10 minutes. Flip the ribs and brush with the reserved marinade. Grill for 8 to 10 minutes more, flipping the ribs about every 2 minutes and brushing on more marinade after each turn. When they're ready, the ribs will be juicy, ruddy from the miso, and the bones will stick out. A bit of char on the surface is okay. Test for doneness using "The 'Nick-and-Peek' Method" (see page 111). Extra-thick ribs might need a few more minutes. Let the ribs rest for 2 minutes and serve.

Garlic–Yuzu Kosho Lamb Chops

The *yuzu kosho* and soy sauce give these fast-grilling lamb chops a zesty Japanese spin. Lamb might not be the first thing you think of as "Japanese food," but there's a long tradition of eating it on the far northern main island of Hokkaido.

Serves 4

2 tablespoons green yuzu kosho (page 7)

10 cloves garlic, finely grated

¹/₂ cup olive oil

2 tablespoons soy sauce

16 lamb chops, each ¹/₂ inch thick (about 2 pounds)

To make the marinade, mix the *yuzu kosho*, grated garlic, olive oil, and soy sauce in a bowl. Pour three-fourths of the marinade into a baking dish or rimmed sheet pan and reserve the rest. Lay each lamb chop in the marinade and flip it 4 times to generously coat on all sides; set aside.

Preheat a grill to medium-hot. Grill the lamb chops for about 1¹/₂ minutes per side to sear them. Brush on the reserved marinade and cook for 1 minute more, flipping once, and brushing on more marinade after you turn. The lamb chops will release a heavenly *yuzu*-garlic fragrance when they're ready. Serve immediately.

Lamb Shoulder Steak
with Japanese Curry Oil

This dish is a favorite of Tadashi's daughters, who, like their dad, love the combination of curry and grilled lamb. The grated garlic and soy sauce in the marinade marry with the curry to add heat and a savory note. *Mitsuba* is a fresh-tasting Japanese herb; if you can't find it, substitute finely chopped parsley or cilantro.

Serves 4

1/2 cup olive oil

2 tablespoons grated garlic

3 tablespoons madras curry powder

4 teaspoons soy sauce

4 lamb shoulder steaks (about 2 pounds)

2 tablespoons chopped mitsuba leaves, for garnish

To make the marinade, whisk together the olive oil, garlic, curry powder, and soy sauce in a bowl. Pour three-fourths of the marinade into a baking dish or sheet pan and reserve the rest. Lay the lamb steaks in the marinade and flip them 4 times to generously coat all over. Marinate the lamb steaks for 1 hour at room temperature.

Preheat a grill to a two-zone fire (medium and hot). Grill the lamb steaks for about 7 minutes this way: Start on hot heat for about 1 minute, then shift the pork to medium heat. After about 2 minutes, flip the steaks and repeat the two-zone grilling on the other side. Once you turn the lamb, brush with the reserved marinade. Grill for 1 more minute on hot heat to caramelize the marinade, flipping the lamb 2 times and brushing with marinade after each turn. When the lamb is ready, it'll be browned and glossy. Test for doneness using "The 'Nick-and-Peek' Method" (see page 111). Let the lamb rest for about 2 minutes. Garnish with the mitsuba leaves and serve.

Calf's Liver with Ginger-Sesame Oil

Calf's liver is a delicacy eaten raw in Japan, dipped into sesame oil and salt, sometimes with grated garlic or ginger mixed in, too. Here we dredge the liver in flour to seal in the juices before dipping into traditional flavorings. Make sure your grill is preheated, and the grate brushed and well oiled, or the liver will stick. Grill quickly to sear, it's okay if the liver is rare on the inside.

Serves 4

1/2 cup all-purpose flour

1/4 cup sesame oil

1 tablespoon grated fresh ginger

2 tablespoons soy sauce

1 teaspoon freshly ground black pepper

4 pieces of calf's liver (1/2 inch thick), about 1 1/2 pounds

Salt

Pour the flour onto a large plate. Ready another plate for the marinated liver.

To make the marinade, mix together the sesame oil, grated ginger, soy sauce, and black pepper in a bowl and pour into a baking dish or rimmed sheet pan. Lightly season the liver with salt on all sides.

For each piece of liver, first dredge in the flour, then lay in the marinade and flip it 3 times to coat all over. Place the coated pieces of liver on the reserved plate.

Preheat a grill to hot. Brush and oil the grate well. Grill the liver for about 3 minutes to sear, turning once. Serve immediately.

VEGETABLES

ONCE YOU GET YOUR FIRE GOING, you'll want to throw a few veggies on the grill to complement your meat, poultry, or fish—or turn the veggies themselves into the stars. Either way, the recipes in this chapter make it easy to grill your greens. While we often think of fish as the signature Japanese food, vegetables follow close behind. Most of Japan is temperate enough to support four growing seasons, and the concept of *shun* (peak season of flavor for vegetables and other foods) is embedded into the cooking. In fact, if you take *shun* into account, you can count over thirty micro-growing seasons in the country. These perfectly harvested veggies find their way into everyday cooking as well as *shojin ryori*, the Buddhist vegetarian cuisine centered in Kyoto, Japan's ancient capital. Kyoto, by the way, is itself an agricultural zone, with historic, heirloom vegetables called *kyo yasai* grown in urban farms that dot the city, and protected by law.

Foil-Baking Veggies on the Grill

Cooking veggies over charcoal has long been a fundamental part of Japanese cuisine, either skewered—like Shiitake Mushrooms (page 42), Asparagus (page 44), or Shishito Peppers (page 43)—or placed directly on the grill. To these methods, we add another option: foil-baking. Why? Simplicity. The foil-baked recipes we include are a snap to prep and throw on the grill, plus you don't have to watch or turn them—so you can focus on your other dishes while they happily cook away on the side. The results, too, are incredible; the flavors inside the foil combine and mingle, and the vegetables themselves transform and caramelize on the fire. We always do a couple of foil-baked dishes whenever we grill. Serve your grilled veggies on platters, so everyone can dig into them, early and often.

All-Purpose Vegetable Marinade in a Hurry

If you're pressed for time, here's a fast and easy marinade to use for almost any vegetable: Mix together equal amounts of soy sauce, lemon juice, and olive oil and brush on mushrooms, zucchini, eggplant, pepper, tomato—you name it—and grill (see Portobello with Freshly Chopped Mitsuba, page 142). This marinade gives veggies a dose of the basics—salt, acid, and umami. You can also give the marinade more zing by adding a touch of *yuzu kosho*, black pepper, white pepper, cayenne pepper, garlic, *shichimi togarashi*, shiso, *sansho*, or thyme. Simple and delicious.

VARIATION Try the all-purpose vegetable marinade as a fast, easy, and heavenly dressing for any leafy green salad.

Whole Grilled Japanese Eggplant with Lemon and Soy Sauce

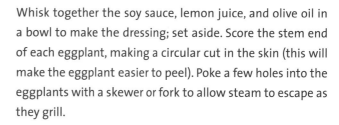

Japanese eggplants have thin skins and few seeds, just meaty, flavorful flesh that transforms into tender, creamy textured, fragrant, smoky goodness when grilled. The classic way to enjoy this dish is with just soy sauce or Ponzu (page 69) and a mound of *katsuobushi*, dried shaved bonito flakes (a type of tuna). The dressing below is more contemporary, but also fantastic. Either way, get your hands on these eggplants and grill them.

Serves 4

2 tablespoons soy sauce

4 teaspoons lemon juice

2 teaspoons olive oil

4 Japanese eggplants (about 1 pound)

¼ cup *katsuobushi*, dried, shaved bonito flakes (a type of tuna), optional

Whisk together the soy sauce, lemon juice, and olive oil in a bowl to make the dressing; set aside. Score the stem end of each eggplant, making a circular cut in the skin (this will make the eggplant easier to peel). Poke a few holes into the eggplants with a skewer or fork to allow steam to escape as they grill.

Preheat a grill to medium. Grill for about 8 minutes, turning the eggplants a quarter turn every 2 minutes. Try to grill the eggplant all around. Test the eggplants for doneness by pressing against their sides with a pair of tongs. If the eggplants give easily, they're ready. Transfer the eggplants to a plate.

As soon as the eggplants are cool enough to handle, carefully peel off the skin (the skin comes off more easily if the eggplant is warm; don't let it cool completely). Once you've removed the skin, remove the stems, and slice each eggplant into 4 pieces, cutting on an angle. Transfer the eggplant slices to a platter. Drizzle with dressing, sprinkle with the bonito, and serve.

Corn Brushed with Soy Sauce and Mirin

Grilled corn is about as all-American as it gets, but Japan has a tradition of eating grilled corn, too—especially at shrine festivals (*matsuri*). During these celebrations, pushcart vendors set up outdoor portable grills on the route to the temple and roast corn basted with soy sauce. There's no way to pass one of these "corn guys" without being instantly smitten by the heavenly aroma coming off their grills. Try it at home, and you'll know what we mean.

Serves 4

3 tablespoons soy sauce
1 tablespoon mirin
4 ears corn, in their husks

Mix together the soy sauce and mirin in a bowl to make the marinade; set aside.

Preheat a grill to medium. Place the corn directly on the grate. Grill for about 20 minutes, turning about every 5 minutes. Transfer the corn to a cutting board. When the husks are cool enough to touch, shuck them. Return the corn to the grill and brush with the marinade. Grill for about 2 more minutes, turning the corn every 30 seconds, and brushing with more marinade. The corn will begin to caramelize and brown; be careful not to burn. Serve immediately.

Asparagus with Miso-Mayonnaise Dipping Sauce

This is a terrific dish for any get-together or party. But don't overlook the variation that follows, a fast and simple everyday way to grill asparagus, which we love, too. You may want to use a wire grid (vegetable grid) to ensure that the asparagus don't fall through the grate.

Serves 4

1/3 cup mayonnaise

1 tablespoon *shiro miso* (savory white miso) (page 6)

1/4 teaspoon shichimi togarashi (page 7)

1 bunch jumbo asparagus (about 1 pound), trimmed

1 tablespoon olive oil

1/4 teaspoon salt

To make the dipping sauce, mix together the mayonnaise, miso, and *shichimi togarashi* in a bowl. Divide between 4 small dipping bowls and set aside.

Lay the asparagus in a single layer on a large plate. Drizzle the olive oil and sprinkle the salt over the asparagus, and use your hands to coat each stalk well.

Preheat a grill to medium. Place the asparagus perpendicular to the bars of the grate, so they don't fall in. Grill for about 4 minutes, turning once. The asparagus should be slightly brown, firm, and just cooked through, but not mushy. Be careful not to burn. Transfer the asparagus to a platter and serve. Dip the asparagus in the flavored mayonnaise to eat.

VARIATION To make Sesame–Soy Sauce Asparagus, instead of preparing the dipping sauce, mix together 1 tablespoon sesame oil, 2 teaspoons soy sauce, and 1/4 teaspoon *shichimi togarashi* in a bowl. Lay the asparagus in a single layer on a large plate. Drizzle the mixture over the asparagus and use your hands to coat each stalk well. Grill as instructed in the main recipe.

Portobello with Freshly Chopped Mitsuba

Here we use our "All-Purpose Vegetable Marinade in a Hurry" (page 138) spiked with freshly ground black pepper, which works perfectly with these meaty, juicy mushrooms. If you can't find mitsuba, a Japanese herb, substitute with 1 tablespoon of chopped parsley or cilantro.

Serves 4

2 tablespoons olive oil

2 tablespoons soy sauce

2 tablespoons freshly squeezed lemon juice

1/2 teaspoon freshly ground black pepper

2 Portobello mushrooms (1/2 to 3/4 pound), stemmed

1 bunch mitsuba, ends trimmed, leaves and stems chopped into 1-inch pieces, for garnish

Whisk together the olive oil, soy sauce, lemon juice, and black pepper in a bowl to make the marinade; pour into a baking dish or rimmed sheet pan. Lay the mushrooms in the mixture and marinate for about 1 minute on each side.

Preheat a grill to medium. Grill for about 6 minutes this way: Start with the cap side down for about 3 minutes, then flip and grill the other side for about 2 minutes. Finish with the cap side down again for about 1 minute, to sear. When they're ready, the mushrooms will be juicy, browned, and lightly charred. Transfer the mushrooms to a cutting board. Cut each portobello in half, then cut each half on an angle into 1-inch slices. Sprinkle the chopped mitsuba over the mushroom slices and serve.

Zucchini with Shiso and Olive Oil

Japanese flavors meld perfectly with this iconic Italian veggie. If you use really fat zucchini (more than 1 inch in diameter), cut them into thick slices instead of lengthwise.

Serves 4

2 large zucchini (about 1 pound), halved lengthwise

¼ cup olive oil

1 bunch shiso (about 10 leaves), finely chopped

2 teaspoons salt

Score the skin of the zucchini by making three equally spaced lengthwise cuts into the skin, about ¼ inch deep.

Mix together the olive oil, shiso leaves, and salt in a bowl to make the marinade; pour into a baking dish or rimmed sheet pan. Roll the zucchini halves in the marinade to generously coat them all over.

Preheat a grill to medium. Grill for about 4 minutes, turning once. Test for doneness by pressing the zucchini with a pair of tongs. If the zucchini give easily, they're ready. Serve immediately.

Tomatoes with Garlic, Sansho, and Olive Oil

Beefsteak or plum tomatoes work great with this recipe—the fresher the tomato, the faster it will cook. The tomato half acts as a cup to hold all the wonderful juices and flavors bubbling inside; use a spoon to scoop out the tender flesh. If the skin burns, don't worry, just don't eat it. This method adapts perfectly to the oven, too. If you can't find *mitsuba*, a Japanese herb, substitute 1 tablespoon of chopped fresh parsley or cilantro.

Serves 4

4 tablespoons olive oil

2 cloves garlic, finely minced

1 tablespoon soy sauce

1 teaspoon sansho (page 7)

1 teaspoon salt

4 medium tomatoes (about 1¼ pounds), halved across the center

1 bunch mitsuba, ends trimmed, leaves and stems chopped into 1-inch pieces, for garnish

Whisk together the olive oil, garlic, soy sauce, *sansho*, and salt in a bowl to make the marinade; pour into a baking dish or rimmed sheet pan. Lay the tomato halves in the marinade, sliced side down. Marinate for about 1 minute.

Preheat a grill to medium. Grill, sliced side down, for about 2 minutes. Turn and grill the tomatoes until you see the insides and juices of the tomato bubbling, about 8 more minutes. As the tomatoes are grilling, spoon the remaining marinade on top. Serve immediately, sprinkled with the chopped mitsuba.

Foil-Baked Mushrooms with Ponzu Butter

Cooking mushrooms with ponzu and butter is enormously popular in Japan, *enoki butter* (yep, Japanglish) a standard at any *izakaya* (eating pub). Here we use a quartet of cultivated Japanese mushrooms, but feel free to mix and match any fungi you fancy, including crimini, Portobello, white button, even chanterelle or *pied de mouton* (hedgehog mushroom), if you're getting fancy. If can't find *maitake* mushrooms, oyster mushrooms make a perfect substitute for them. Finally, the lime slices in the recipe are there to add fragrance and flavor; you don't eat them.

Serves 4

1/4 cup Ponzu (page 69)

1/2 teaspoon salt

1/2 teaspoon shichimi togarashi (page 7)

4 large shiitake mushrooms (about 4 ounces), stems pulled off and broken in half by hand

5 ounces maitake (hen-of-the-woods) mushrooms, ends trimmed and stalks separated

1 (3 1/2-ounce) package shimeji mushrooms, ends trimmed and stalks separated

1 (3 1/2-ounce) package enoki mushrooms, ends trimmed and stalks separated

1/4 lime, cut into thin slices

2 tablespoons unsalted butter, cut into small chunks

Cut a 3-foot-long piece of heavy-duty aluminum foil; fold in half lengthwise and set aside. Mix together the ponzu, salt, and *shichimi togarashi* in a large bowl. Add the shiitake, *maitake, shimeji*, and enoki mushrooms and gently toss together with the ponzu mixture until all the mushrooms are coated.

Transfer the mixture of mushrooms the aluminum foil sheet, arranging in a mound in the center of the foil. Lay the lime slices over the mushrooms and randomly scatter chunks of butter on top. Carefully fold one end of the aluminum foil over the other and pinch the sides to close, creating a neat pouch.

Preheat a grill to medium-hot. Place the aluminum foil pouch directly on the grate and grill for about 10 minutes. Carefully open the pouch slightly to peek inside and check if the mushrooms are cooked through and sizzling (be careful of escaping steam).

Transfer the foil pouch to a plate, unwrap it, and push the lime slices to the side (you don't eat them). Serve the mushrooms directly from the pouch.

Foil-Baked Edamame

Edamame are soybeans, usually sold frozen. But sometimes farmer's markets in communities with large Asian populations sell fresh edamame (even still on the stalk). If you can find them, grab the fresh ones: the taste is wonderful.

Serves 4

1 pound bag frozen edamame, thawed

1 tablespoon soy sauce

1 teaspoon salt

Cut a 3-foot-long piece of heavy-duty aluminum foil and fold in half lengthwise. Place the edamame on the center of the aluminum foil sheet, arranging in a mound in the center. Drizzle the soy sauce over the beans and and sprinkle with salt. Carefully fold one end of the aluminum foil over the other and pinch the sides to close, creating a neat pouch.

Preheat a grill to medium-hot. Place the aluminum foil pouch directly on the grate and grill for about 5 minutes. Transfer the foil pouch to a plate and carefully open it (be careful of escaping steam). Mix the edamame to combine the flavors and serve directly from the foil pouch.

Foil-Baked Green Beans with Soy Sauce and Garlic

Make sure not to overcook the green beans. You want them firm and crunchy, not mushy like hospital food. Mix together the green beans just before serving to evenly coat all of them with the fragrant marinade. These beans taste great room temperature or even cold (a perfect leftover for the next day).

Serves 4

1 pound green beans, ends snapped off, and beans cut in half on an angle

1 clove garlic, finely minced or pressed

1 tablespoon finely chopped yellow onion

2 tablespoons soy sauce

2 tablespoons sake

2 tablespoons olive oil

1/2 teaspoon salt

Cut a 3-foot-long piece of heavy-duty aluminum foil; fold in half lengthwise and set aside. Toss together all the ingredients in a bowl to make the marinade. Transfer the green bean mixture to the aluminum foil sheet, arranging in a mound in the center. Carefully fold one end of the aluminum foil over the other and pinch the sides to close, creating a neat pouch.

Preheat a grill to medium-hot. Place the aluminum foil pouch directly on the grate and grill for about 10 minutes. Carefully open the pouch slightly to peek inside and check if the green beans are cooked through and sizzling (be careful of escaping steam). Transfer the foil pouch to a plate and unwrap it. Serve the green beans directly from the pouch.

Foil-Baked Onions with Soy Sauce

The beauty of grilling whole onions this way is that they almost magically transform from sharp to irresistibly caramelized and sweet. The soy sauce enhances the natural flavor of the onions to make them even more delicious.

Serves 4

2 medium Spanish onions (about 2 pounds), halved across the center

¼ cup soy sauce

Cut four 12-inch-long pieces of heavy-duty aluminum foil and fold each in half. Liberally brush each onion half with soy sauce, and place on foil, cut side down. Fold over the foil to wrap the onions completely.

Preheat a grill to medium. Place the foil-wrapped onions directly on the grate. Grill for about 35 minutes, turning the onions after about 10 minutes, and again after about 20 minutes. Test the onions for doneness by pressing the sides with tongs. If the onions give easily, they're ready. Unwrap the onions and serve.

Foil-Baked Garlic with Miso

As with whole onions, grilling a head of garlic transforms the cloves within from sharp to caramelized, sweet, and tender, with a texture like a cooked potato. The miso adds a layer of savory flavor and also caramelizes as it grills.

Serves 4

2 heads garlic (with papery peel intact), halved across the center

1 tablespoon *shiro miso* (savory white miso) (page 6)

Cut four 12-inch-long pieces of heavy-duty aluminum foil and fold each in half. On each piece of aluminum foil, place a half-head of garlic, cut side down. Spread the miso in a thin layer over the cut side of the garlic, bunch the foil together to close it.

Preheat a grill to medium. Place the foil-wrapped packages directly on the grate, seam side up. Grill for about 12 minutes, turning once. Unwrap and serve.

Foil-Baked Sweet Potatoes with Salt

Roasted sweet potatoes are a favorite snack in Japan. In the old days, pushcart vendors would ply neighborhoods selling these piping-hot tubers. They grilled them by sticking the sweet potatoes inside a pile of hot pebbles and firing from underneath with gas or charcoal. These vendors are mostly gone now, but Tadashi remembers them from his childhood in Tokyo, when they rang a sonorous bell to announce their arrival (and trigger a Pavlovian response from everyone in the neighborhood). Japanese sweet potatoes have pale yellow flesh and are denser and more delicately sweet than other varieties. But this method works great with any kind of sweet potato (remember, a sweet potato is distinct from a yam—two different kinds of tubers). Scoop out the flesh with a spoon or chopsticks to eat the entire sweet potato, skin and all.

Serves 4

2 large sweet potatoes (about 2 pounds), halved lengthwise

Salt

Cut four 12-inch-long pieces of heavy-duty aluminum foil and fold each in half. On each piece of aluminum foil, place a sweet potato half. Fold over the aluminum foil to wrap the sweet potatoes completely.

Preheat a grill to medium. Place the foil-wrapped sweet potatoes directly on the grate. Grill for about 1 hour, turning the sweet potatoes a quarter turn about every 10 minutes, to make sure the entire sweet potato is cooked through. Test the sweet potato for doneness by pressing the sides with tongs. If the sweet potato gives easily, it's ready. Unwrap the sweet potatoes (be careful of escaping steam) and serve. Sprinkle salt on top to taste.

Foil-Baked Carrots with Salt

If you're like us, you usually have a few carrots lying around in the fridge. Here's our suggestion: The next time you grill, slap 'em on the grate. This simple method will transform carrots into something incredible.

Serves 4

**4 medium carrots
(about 1 pound)**

Salt

Cut four 12-inch-long pieces of heavy-duty aluminum foil and fold each in half. On each piece of aluminum foil, place a whole carrot. Fold over the aluminum foil to wrap the carrots completely.

Preheat a grill to medium. Place the foil-wrapped carrots directly on the grate. Grill the carrots for about 20 minutes, turning 2 or 3 times. Test the carrots for doneness by pressing the sides with tongs. If the carrots give easily, they're ready.

Unwrap the carrots (be careful of any escaping steam). When they're just cool enough to touch, peel off the skin, which will slide off easily, and serve. Sprinkle salt on top to taste.

Foil-Wrapped Taro Root

Japanese taro are about the size and shape of an egg, with a hairy brown skin. They have a sticky consistency when raw, but grilling turns the flesh tender, fluffy, and delicious.

Serves 4

4 medium-to-large Japanese taro roots (about 1 pound), washed well and halved lengthwise

Salt

Cut four 4-inch-long pieces of heavy-duty aluminum foil. On each piece of aluminum foil, place a piece of taro root, sliced side down. Fold the aluminum foil to wrap the vegetables completely.

Preheat a grill to medium. Grill the taro roots about 16 minutes, turning once. Test for doneness by pressing the sides of the taro with tongs. If the taro gives easily, it's done. Unwrap the taro (watch for escaping steam), and serve immediately. Sprinkle with salt to taste.

YAKI ONIGIRI

AS ANY JAPANESE KID, or former kid, can tell you, *onigiri* are rice balls, the versatile national snack found in homes, convenience stores, and every school lunchbox. These balls are typically stuffed, mixed, or sprinkled on the outside with a multitude of tasty flavorings. They're also typically formed into oval or triangular shapes, despite being called "balls." *Onigiri* go way back in history; people in Japan ate rice balls over a thousand years ago, before chopsticks became common. Samurai carried o*nigiri* wrapped in bamboo leaves to fortify themselves during battle; there's mention of *onigiri* enjoyed at picnics in an eleventh-century diary. In Japan today, *onigiri* are still the go-to food for picnics, or any outdoor or on-the-run eating, for that matter. It's not surprising that they started being grilled, too, which is what *yaki onigiri* are—grilled rice balls. Fire crisps up and caramelizes the rice on the outside, creating a delicious crust, which makes them even more irresistible. Below, we share six classic varieties of *yaki onigiri* that we love.

How to Cook Japanese Rice

There are two basic ways to prepare Japanese rice: rice cooker or stovetop. If you have an electronic rice cooker, wash and rest the rice as we describe below, then follow cooker instructions. To prepare rice on the stovetop, an enameled cast-iron or cast-iron pot works best because these heavy pots do such a great job distributing heat.

MAKES 4 CUPS OF RICE

> 2 cups Japanese short-grain white rice
>
> 2 cups water

Wash the rice to remove surface starch by placing the rice in a bowl, filling it with water, and swirling the rice with your hand. Drain off the milky liquid. Repeat 3 or 4 times until the water becomes clear enough to see the rice. Wash quickly; the entire process should take no longer than 3 minutes (soaking the rice in the washing water too long can cloud its flavor). Strain the rice into a colander, cover it with a clean kitchen towel, and let it rest for 15 minutes, so the grains naturally rehydrate, which helps them cook evenly.

Add the rice and 2 cups of water to a pot. Cover and bring to a boil over high heat. Decrease the heat to medium and cook 10 minutes, until you smell a beautiful rice aroma in the steam escaping from the pot. Be careful not to overcook, or you'll burn the rice. Turn off the heat and let the covered pot sit for 10 minutes, a critical step that completes the cooking process. Uncover the pot, gently stir the rice with a large spoon to fluff it up, and it's ready.

HOW TO MAKE YAKI ONIGIRI

Use 1 cup of hot (or warm) cooked Japanese short grain rice per serving. Add the rice to a small bowl (like a cereal bowl) just big enough to hold it. Jiggle the bowl, moving it in a flat, circular motion, like the motion of a hula hoop, until the rice forms into a ball on its own—a neat kitchen trick Tadashi's mom taught him. This motion packs the rice so it holds together when it grills.

Wet your hands and place the ball of rice between your cupped palms. Now squeeze, flip, and turn the rice ball several times to form it into a triangular shape. This motion takes a little practice, but after a few *yaki onigiri*, you'll get the hang of it. Make sure not to compact the rice too tight; you want it to just stick together.

Grill *yaki onigiri* over medium heat. If the fire's too hot, the rice will burn. We like to place the *yaki onigiri* along the cooler edges of a grill while other foods cook in the hotter center. Watch the rice carefully while it grills; perfect *yaki onigiri* need constant attention.

Soy Sauce Yaki Onigiri

Serves 4

4 cups cooked rice, formed into 4 onigiri (see "How to Make Yaki Onigiri," page 156)

¼ cup soy sauce

Preheat a grill to medium. Grill the *onigiri* for about 6 minutes, flipping once. Brush the *onigiri* with the soy sauce. Grill for about 2 minutes more, flipping every 30 seconds, and brushing on more soy sauce after each turn. Grill the edges of the *onigiri* triangle, too, about 20 seconds per edge. The *onigiri* will have a crispy, caramelized crust when they're done. Serve immediately.

Miso Yaki Onigiri

Serves 4

¼ cup red miso (page 6)

¼ cup water

4 cups cooked rice, formed into onigiri (see "How to Make Yaki Onigiri," page 156)

Mix together the miso and water in a bowl and set aside.

Preheat a grill to medium. Grill the *onigiri* for about 6 minutes, turning once. Brush the *onigiri* with the miso. Grill for about 2 minutes more, flipping every 30 seconds, and brushing on more miso after each turn. Grill the edges of the *onigiri* triangle, too, about 20 seconds per edge. The *onigiri* will have a crispy, caramelized crust when they're done. Serve immediately.

VARIATION You can add 1 tablespoon finely chopped scallions, or 1 teaspoon finely chopped garlic, *sansho, shichimi togarashi,* or *tobanjan,* to add another flavor note to the miso.

Shiso-Ume Yaki Onigiri

Serves 4

4 cups cooked rice

1 bunch shiso (about 10 leaves), finely chopped

¼ cup ume paste

1 tablespoon water

Gently mix together the rice and shiso leaves in a bowl. Form into onigiri (see "How to Make Yaki Onigiri," page 156). Mix together the *ume* paste and the 1 tablespoon water in a bowl and set aside.

Preheat a grill to medium. Grill the *onigiri* for about 6 minutes, turning once. Brush the *onigiri* with the thinned *ume* paste. Grill for about 2 minutes more, flipping every 30 seconds, and brushing on more *ume* paste after each turn. Grill the edges of the onigiri triangle, too, about 20 seconds per edge. The *onigiri* will have a pink-tinged, crispy, caramelized crust when they're done. Serve immediately.

Yukari Shiso Salt Yaki Onigiri

Yukari shiso salt is powdered dried purple shiso leaves mixed with salt, a tangy and colorful seasoning. It's often available in Japanese markets, but if you have trouble finding it, substitute another flavored Japanese salt like *matcha* salt (green tea salt) or *furikake*, seasoning for rice that comes in many varieties.

Serves 4

4 cups cooked rice

4 teaspoons yakari shiso salt

Gently mix together the rice and *yukari shiso* salt in a bowl. Form into *onigiri* (see "How to Make Yaki Onigiri," page 156).

Preheat a grill to medium. Grill the *onigiri* for about 8 minutes, turning twice. Grill the edges of the *onigiri* triangle, too, about 20 seconds per edge. The *onigiri* will have a crispy, caramelized crust when they're done. Serve immediately.

Ao Nori Seaweed and Sesame Yaki Onigiri

Ao nori is powdered nori seaweed that hasn't been roasted and is usually sold in a can or a pack. (Nori are the papery seaweed sheets that are used to wrap sushi rolls.)

Serves 4

4 cups cooked rice

4 teaspoons ao nori

4 teaspoons roasted white sesame seed

Salt

Gently mix together the rice, ao nori, and sesame seed in a bowl. To form into *onigiri*, wet your hands, sprinkle them with salt, then form the rice mixture into *onigiri* (see "How to Make Yaki Onigiri," page 156). (This will add enough salt to the *onigiri*.)

Preheat a grill to medium. Grill the *onigiri* for about 8 minutes, turning twice. Grill the edges of the *onigiri* triangle, too, about 20 seconds per edge. The *onigiri* will have a crispy, caramelized crust when they're done. Serve immediately.

Bonito Flakes–Black Sesame Yaki Onigiri

You can substitute white sesame seed for the black or use a mixture of both.

Serves 4

4 cups cooked rice

1 packed cup *katsuobushi*, dried shaved bonito flakes (a type of tuna), chopped fine

5 teaspoons roasted black sesame seed

¼ cup soy sauce

Gently mix together the rice, bonito, and sesame seed in a bowl. Form into *onigiri* (see "How to Make Yaki Onigiri," page 156).

Preheat a grill to medium. Grill the *onigiri* for about 6 minutes, flipping once. Brush the *onigiri* with the soy sauce. Grill for about 2 minutes more, flipping every 30 seconds, and brushing on more soy sauce after each turn. Grill the edges of the *onigiri* triangle, too, about 20 seconds per edge. The *onigiri* will have a crispy, caramelized crust when they're done. Serve immediately.

PERFECT SIDE DISHES

YOU'LL NOTICE A COUPLE OF THINGS about the dishes in this chapter. First, they all feature vegetables as the main attraction, often leafy ones. And second, they're all bright, light, and vinegary. There's a reason for this: these side dishes are meant to offer a refreshing counterpoint to the richness of the grilled meat, poultry, and fish recipes in the book. Make sure to prepare at least a couple of them when you plan a Japanese grill meal. And, like our vegetable dishes (see "Vegetables," page 137 serve them on platters, so family and friends can dig in at will to refresh their palates and balance all that protein coming off the fiery coals. We love these dishes, which are a selection of traditional Japanese favorites and contemporary inspirations Tadashi whips up for his family whenever he fires the barbecue.

Wafu Dressing

This is our all-purpose Japanese salad dressing and not just for grill time. It's perfect for any leafy salad and can sit in the fridge for up to 1 month—so we always keep some on hand. (Just mix or whisk well before using it again.) The dressing is based on a traditional Japanese vinegar preparation called *tosazu*, but when you add oil and lemon juice it morphs into *wafu*— "Japanese-style," and, in this case, vinaigrette. The beauty of *wafu* dressing, too, is that you can easily enhance it with almost any accent, including ginger, garlic, wasabi, *karashi* mustard, *yuzu kosho*, *tobanjan*, *shichimi togarashi*, *sansho*, black pepper, and cayenne pepper. Create your own dressing with these accents or use the terrific *wafu* variations in the recipes that follow.

Makes about 2½ cups

1 cup Japanese rice vinegar

1 cup water

¼ cup mirin

¼ cup soy sauce

1 tablespoon sugar

1 teaspoon salt

½ cup tightly packed *katsuobushi*, dried shaved bonito flakes (a type of tuna)

2 tablespoons sesame oil

1 tablespoon vegetable oil

1 tablespoon freshly squeezed lemon juice

Add the vinegar, the 1 cup water, mirin, soy sauce, sugar, salt, and bonito flakes to a saucepan and bring it to a boil over medium heat. Remove from the heat and let the mixture steep for 10 minutes. Strain through cheesecloth or a fine mesh sieve, gently pressing the flakes to release more liquid (don't press too hard). Let the liquid come to room temperature. Whisk in the sesame oil, vegetable oil, and lemon juice. Use as desired.

VARIATION Quick Wafu Dressing: Here's a simpler, faster version of our *wafu* dressing; it isn't as complex and flavorful as the full recipe, but it works perfectly in a pinch: Whisk together ½ cup Japanese rice vinegar, 2 tablespoons soy sauce, 1 tablespoon sugar, 1 tablespoon sesame oil, and 2 tablespoons vegetable oil to make about ¾ cup. Use in the recipes that follow.

Watercress Salad
with Karashi Mustard Wafu Dressing

This is a classic pairing: the spiciness of watercress leaves meets the heat of Japanese *karashi* mustard. The cucumber and radish add nice crunch and color. If you can find them, use drier Japanese, Kirby, Persian, or English (seedless) cucumbers for this dish. Hothouse cucumbers work nicely, too.

Serves 4

2 bunches watercress (about 11 ounces)

1 small cucumber (about 2 ounces)

Salt

5 small red radishes, thinly sliced

³/₄ cup Wafu Dressing (page 162)

2 teaspoons karashi mustard

1 teaspoon sesame seed

Trim and discard the thick stems of the watercress and slice the leafy parts across the centers to make them bite size. Fill a bowl with cold water and add the watercress. Soak for 10 minutes to crisp the leaves. Drain well in a colander and set aside.

Rub the skin of the cucumber with salt to remove its bitterness, then rinse under cold running water. Slice the unpeeled cucumber into thin coins and set aside.

Whisk together the dressing and mustard in a bowl large enough to hold the entire salad.

To assemble the salad, add the watercress leaves, cucumber and radish slices to the bowl with the dressing and gently toss until the watercress leaves are evenly coated with dressing. Transfer to a platter, sprinkle the sesame seed, and serve.

Tomato-Shiso Salad with Garlic Wafu Dressing

We love beefsteak tomatoes for this salad, but feel free to mix and match different varieties and colors, including heirlooms. Just make sure to use the ripest tomatoes possible.

Serves 4

1/2 cup Wafu Dressing (page 162)

1 clove garlic, finely chopped

1/4 teaspoon shichimi togarashi (page 7)

1 pound ripe tomatoes, cut into 1/4-inch-thick slices

2 tablespoons finely chopped yellow onion

3 bunches shiso leaves (about 30 leaves), sliced into long, thin strips (chiffonade)

Whisk together the dressing, garlic, and *shichimi togarashi* in a bowl; set aside.

Arrange the tomato slices in one layer on a platter. Drizzle the dressing over the tomato, then sprinkle the onion over them. Place the sliced shiso leaves in a clump in the center of the platter and serve. Eat the tomato together with the shiso.

Wakame Salad with Ginger Wafu Dressing

We love wakame for its delicate briny flavor and tender, silky texture. Make sure you mix the dressing in this recipe very well before you pour it on the *wakame*, so it coats the seaweed evenly. If you can't find the *negi* called for in the recipe, substitute two (4-inch) lengths of the white part of a scallion.

Serves 4

1 cup dried wakame seaweed

4-inch-length negi, white part only (about 2 ounces)

³/₄ cup Wafu Dressing (page 162)

1 teaspoon grated fresh ginger

1 small red radish, thinly sliced

1 teaspoon toasted sesame seed, for garnish

Fill a bowl large enough to allow the *wakame* to expand with cold water and add the *wakame*. Soak until the *wakame* rehydrates, about 10 minutes. Drain the *wakame* in a colander, gently squeezing the seaweed to remove excess water.

Halve the *negi* lengthwise, then slice each half, lengthwise, as thinly as possible. Fill a bowl with cold water and add the sliced *negi*. Soak for about 5 minutes to crisp them up. Drain the *negi* slices and pat dry them with a paper towel.

Make the dressing by whisking together the *wafu* dressing and the grated ginger in a bowl.

To assemble the salad, place the *wakame* in a serving bowl in a mound. Randomly toss the negi and radish over the wakame. Pour the dressing on top (the dressing can pool in the bowl). Garnish with sesame seed and serve.

Sea Vegetables

Sea vegetables are an important part of the Japanese diet, loaded with vitamins and minerals. One of the most popular is called *wakame*, a nutritious seaweed used in soups and salads (like our Wakame Salad with Ginger Wafu Dressing, above). *Wakame* is sold dried and can last in your cupboard indefinitely, so it's a convenient ingredient to keep handy. When you reconstitute it, make sure you use a bowl large enough for the *wakame* to expand.

Onion Salad with Soy Sauce and Bonito

You'll often find this salad at yakitori joints, because the sharpness of the onions mellows the richness of all those delectable skewers. If it works with grilled chicken on a stick, why not pair it with any other grilled meat, fish, or poultry? Fast and simple to whip up, onion salad is one of our standard side dishes. You'll be amazed how good it is. Use a hand-held food slicer or mandolin to make cutting the onion easier.

Serves 4

1 medium Spanish onion (about ³/₄ pound), halved lengthwise (stem to root end)

¹/₄ cup soy sauce

1 tablespoon sesame oil

1¹/₂ cups loosely packed katsuobushi, dried shaved bonito flakes (a type of tuna)

Cut off the root ends of the onion and remove the peel. Slice the onion halves as thinly as possible across the grain. Fill a large bowl with cold water and add the slices to the water. Soak for 15 minutes to crisp the onion and mellow its sharpness. Drain the slices in a colander, shaking out as much water as possible.

To assemble the salad, pile the onion slices in a mound on a platter. Using a large spoon, drizzle the soy sauce in concentric circles over the onions to evenly dress them. Drizzle the sesame oil over the onions in the same way. Roughly pile the bonito on top of the onions and serve. Toss the ingredients to eat.

Green Cabbage Salad
with Carrot-Ginger Vinaigrette

Like onions, cabbage is another vegetable typically found in yakitori joints, except that it's served plain, without any dressing—the crunchy leaves are a refreshing counterpoint to the meaty skewers. In this dish we thinly slice the cabbage, and add a flavorful, vinegar-spiked dressing. The cabbage serves the same purpose, but now the flavors are more interesting. If you like, you can substitute savoy or purple cabbage, or romaine, Boston, or iceberg lettuce for the green cabbage. Also, try this tangy vinaigrette with other salads; it's versatile and delicious.

Serves 4

³/₄ pound green cabbage

¹/₂ cup Japanese rice vinegar

2 tablespoons soy sauce

1 tablespoon sugar

1 teaspoon grated fresh ginger

1 tablespoon sesame oil

1 medium carrot (about 4 ounces), trimmed, peeled, and thinly sliced

¹/₄ cup thinly sliced onion (about 2 ounces)

Core the cabbage and slice it as thinly as possible (with a sharp knife or hand-held food slicer or mandolin, if you prefer). Fill a large bowl with cold water and add the sliced cabbage. Soak for 5 minutes to crisp the cabbage.

Add the vinegar, soy sauce, sugar, ginger, sesame oil, carrot, and onion to the jar of a blender. Cover and pulse on high speed until smooth, about 1 minute.

To assemble the salad, drain the cabbage in a colander, shaking out as much water as possible. To serve, pile the sliced cabbage in a mound on a platter, pour the dressing on top, and serve. Mix the ingredients to eat.

Daikon Salad with Dried Tiny Shrimp

A large white Japanese radish, daikon is eaten cooked or raw, as it is here. This is a traditional Japanese preparation and a poetic one, too—the daikon leaves sliced the way we describe below resemble gingko leaves, a nice touch. Look for the tiny dried shrimp at any Asian market, not only Japanese ones.

Serves 4

3 tablespoons dried tiny shrimp

1 pound daikon

$1/2$ teaspoon salt

$1/4$ teaspoon shichimi togarashi (page 7)

1 tablespoon finely chopped fresh chives

Preheat a dry skillet over medium heat. When the skillet is hot, add the dried shrimp, cooking and stirring until the shrimp turn deeper pink and releases their fragrance, about 1 minute. Stir constantly; you want to toast the shrimp, but not burn them. Transfer the shrimp to a plate and set aside to cool.

Peel the daikon, making sure to remove its thick white skin to expose its glossy flesh. Quarter the peeled daikon. Slice each quarter as thinly as possible (with a sharp knife or hand-held food slicer or mandolin if you prefer).

To assemble the salad, add the daikon slices, dried shrimp, salt, *shichimi togarashi*, and chives to a bowl and gently mix the ingredients together. Transfer to a platter and serve.

Spinach with Ground Sesame

Here's how you get your kids to love spinach—serve this Japanese home-cooking standard. This spinach preparation is an ideal match to grilled dishes, but is also a perfect side dish for any meal. You can grind the sesame seed with a food processor. But if you live near a Japanese market, pick up a convenient (and inexpensive) sesame-seed hand grinder; you turn it like a pepper mill, and it makes pulverizing seeds a snap. Once you taste this salad, we know you'll be happy you have the grinder.

Serves 4

1 pound fresh spinach, washed well, ends trimmed

$2/3$ cup sesame seed

1 tablespoon sugar

2 tablespoons soy sauce

1 tablespoon sesame oil

Fill a large pot with water and bring it to a boil over high heat. When the water is boiling, add the spinach and blanch until the leaves turn bright green, about 30 seconds. Set a colander in a bowl large enough to hold it. Let the spinach drain in the colander under cold running water. Rinse the spinach for about 1 minute, until it cools (the bowl will fill with water that's okay). Bunch the spinach into a ball and squeeze it to remove the excess water. Set aside.

Place the sesame seed in the work bowl of a food processor fitted with the metal blade. Cover and pulse for about 1 minute to grind the sesame seed to the consistency of cornmeal (don't grind the seed too fine).

To assemble the salad, mix together the ground sesame seed, sugar, soy sauce, and sesame oil in a large bowl. Add the spinach and gently toss until the leaves are evenly coated with the dressing. Transfer to a platter and serve.

VARIATION This sesame dressing pairs well with asparagus, green beans, any kind of leafy cooked green, broccoli, cauliflower, and fiddlehead fern.

Spinach-Bacon Salad with Creamy Tofu Dressing

Here's another take on spinach, albeit a more contemporary one. If it reminds you of a classic spinach salad with bacon and blue cheese dressing, well, guess what inspired Tadashi to come up with this recipe? But instead of a cheesy dressing, the tofu, ginger, soy sauce, and sesame oil give this salad a lighter, more nuanced Japanese sensibility.

Serves 4

1/4 pound sliced bacon

1/2 package silken tofu (about 1/2 pound)

1 teaspoon grated fresh ginger

3 tablespoons Japanese rice vinegar

1 tablespoon soy sauce

2 teaspoons sugar

1 tablespoon sesame oil

1/2 pound fresh spinach, stems trimmed, washed well, and dried

1/2 tablespoon finely chopped scallions (white and green parts)

Line a plate with paper towels and set aside. Preheat a large skillet over medium heat. When the skillet is hot, add the bacon and cook until crisp, about 5 minutes. Transfer the bacon to the paper towel–lined plate to drain. When the bacon has cooled, crumble it into tiny pieces in a bowl and set aside.

To make the dressing, add the tofu, ginger, rice vinegar, soy sauce, sugar, and sesame oil to the jar of a blender. Cover and pulse on high speed until smooth, about 30 seconds.

To assemble the salad, arrange the spinach on a platter. Pour the dressing over the leaves. Sprinkle the crumbled bacon and chopped scallions on top and serve. Mix the ingredients to eat.

Pickled Lotus Root

Lotus root has a delightful crunchy texture and fresh flavor that emerges with blanching. We pickle the lotus with a traditional Japanese vinegar preparation called *amazu*, which gives it a refreshing sweet-and-sour flavor (plus a touch of heat from the chilies). You can also use *amazu* to dress a salad of *wakame* (see Wakame Salad with Ginger Wafu Dressing, page 165) and sliced cucumbers, or drizzle over halved and cooled boiled baby potatoes.

Serves 4

1 cup Japanese rice vinegar, plus 2 tablespoons for blanching the lotus root

1 cup water

1/4 cup sugar

2 teaspoons salt

3 whole dried Japanese chilies (*togarashi*)

3-inch-long piece kombu (a type of naturally preserved kelp)

1 pound fresh lotus root

To make the pickling liquid, prepare an ice bath and set aside. Combine the 1 cup vinegar, 1 cup water, sugar, salt, chilies, and kombu in a saucepan and bring it to a boil over high heat. As soon as the liquid boils, transfer the saucepan to the ice bath to cool. Once it's cool to the touch, pour the pickling liquid into a large bowl and set aside.

Peel the lotus root and cut it into 1/8-inch-thick slices. Place the slices in large bowl filled with cold water and soak for 15 minutes to remove excess surface starch. Strain the lotus root, transfer to a saucepan, and cover with water. Add the remaining 2 tablespoons of vinegar to preserve the white color of the lotus root. Place the saucepan over high heat and bring it to a boil. Boil the lotus root for 1 minute to blanch. Drain in a colander, shaking well to remove any excess water. Let the lotus root cool for about 2 minutes.

Once the lotus root has cooled slightly, add it to the reserved pickling liquid. Marinate at room temperature for at least 2 hours (12 hours, or overnight, is ideal). Once marinated, serve the lotus root slices in the pickling liquid at room temperature.

Arugula-Jako Salad
with Soy Sauce Vinaigrette

Kurozu, an artisan-made rice vinegar that's aged in earthenware jars under the hot sun of Japan's far south, adds a mellow, complex flavor to the vinaigrette. If you can't find this wonderful ingredient, substitute with a good-quality sherry vinegar. *Chirimen jako* are tiny dried baby anchovies no larger than an inch long, which keep in the freezer for months. Toasting them makes the *jako* delightfully crispy, a nice touch. You can also use the soy sauce vinaigrette with other leafy salads.

Serves 4

1/4 cup chirimen jako

2 tablespoons aged Japanese rice vinegar or sherry vinegar

1 tablespoon soy sauce

2 tablespoons extra-virgin olive oil

2 tablespoons finely chopped scallions (white and green parts)

1/4 teaspoon sansho (page 7)

4 cups loosely packed fresh baby arugula

2 red radishes, thinly sliced

1 tablespoon finely chopped fresh chives

Preheat a dry skillet over medium heat. When the skillet is hot, add the *chirimen jako*, cooking and stirring until the *chirimen jako* toasts and turns golden, releasing its fragrance, about 1 minute. Stir constantly; be careful not to burn the fish. Transfer the *chirimen jako* to a plate to cool for at least 5 minutes.

To make the vinaigrette, whisk together the vinegar, soy sauce, olive oil, scallions, and *sansho* in a bowl.

To assemble the salad, arrange the arugula on a platter. Drizzle the vinaigrette over the leaves. Sprinkle *chirimen jako*, radish, and chives on top and serve.

Spicy Bean Sprouts

Besides being an Ono family favorite, this is the easiest recipe in the book: boil, cool, dress, and serve. It doesn't get any simpler than that. *Rayu* is Japanese chili oil; use less of it if you prefer your foods less spicy. If you can't find *rayu*, substitute 2 teaspoons of sesame oil and 1 teaspoon of *shichimi togarashi*.

Serves 4

1 pound bean sprouts

1 tablespoon soy sauce

2 teaspoons rayu (Japanese chili oil)

2 teaspoons sesame seed

Add the bean sprouts to a large pot, cover with water, and bring to a boil over high heat; boil for 30 seconds. Drain the bean sprouts in a colander and let the bean sprouts come to room temperature. Place the bean sprouts in a large bowl and add the soy sauce, *rayu*, and sesame seed. Mix the ingredients together. Transfer to a platter and serve.

Romaine Hearts with Miso-Mustard Dressing

This is a great party dish. The romaine hearts are easy to eat: Hold a spear by the stem and munch on it like corn on the cob. This recipe works perfectly with endive, too.

Serves 4

1 tablespoon pine nuts

¹/₂ pound romaine hearts

¹/₄ cup shiro miso (white savory miso, page 6)

1 tablespoon Dijon mustard

2 tablespoons Japanese rice vinegar

2 tablespoons water

2 teaspoons sugar

2 tablespoons olive oil

2 teaspoons chopped fresh chives (or scallions)

To toast the pine nuts, preheat a dry skillet over medium heat. When the skillet is hot, add the pine nuts, cooking and stirring until the pine nuts turn golden and release their fragrance, about 1 minute. Stir constantly; be careful not to burn the nuts. Transfer the pine nuts to a cutting board and coarsely chop; set aside.

Clean the romaine hearts, removing any limp outside leaves and trimming the stems. Cut them into quarters lengthwise. On a large platter, line up the spears in a row in one layer; set aside.

To make the dressing, add the miso, mustard, vinegar, the 2 tablespoons water, sugar, and olive oil to the jar of a blender. Cover and pulse on high speed until smooth, about 30 seconds.

To assemble the salad, pour the dressing over the romaine hearts. Sprinkle with pine nuts and chives and serve.

Crudités with Three Dipping Sauces

Use a variety of raw vegetables for the crudités. Besides the ones we list below, feel free to use cauliflower, green beans, bell peppers, celery, chilled boiled baby potatoes, daikon, or jicama. *Ishiri* is an ancient Japanese sauce made from fermented squid that adds wonderful, tangy flavor; in fact, it's an ancient cousin of Vietnamese and Thai *nam pla* fish sauce. If you can't find it, substitute *nam pla* or finely chopped anchovies.

Serves 4

MISO-GARLIC DIPPING SAUCE

3 tablespoons red miso (page 6)

2 tablespoons water

1 teaspoon tobanjan (page 7)

2 teaspoons sugar

1/2 clove garlic, finely chopped

1 teaspoon sesame oil

SPICY YUZU MAYONNAISE DIPPING SAUCE

1/2 cup mayonnaise

1 tablespoon red yuzu kosho (page 7)

2 teaspoons soy sauce

ISHIRI-CHIVE MAYONNAISE DIPPING SAUCE

1/2 cup mayonnaise

1 tablespoon ishiri sauce (Japanese fish sauce)

1 teaspoon green yuzu kosho (page 7)

2 tablespoons finely chopped fresh chives (or finely chopped scallions)

CRUDITÉS

6 ounces daikon (large white Japanese radish), peeled, halved lengthwise, and sliced into 1/4-inch-thick half moons

1 medium carrot (about 4 ounces), peeled and quartered lengthwise

1 medium cucumber (about 4 ounces), peeled and quartered lengthwise

5 medium asparagus (about 5 ounces), ends trimmed

1/2 cup cherry tomatoes, stemmed

1/4 pound broccoli florets

For each dipping sauce, add all the ingredients to a bowl and whisk them together until smooth. Transfer the dipping sauces to three serving bowls (for all to share) and set aside.

To assemble the salad, arrange the vegetables on a large platter. Serve alongside the three dipping sauces.

Tofu Salad à la Provençal

Tofu and anchovy? Not the first food pairing that comes to mind, we admit, but we urge you to try it in this colorful, summery salad, another perfect party dish. The creamy sweetness of tofu balances the strong taste of anchovy surprisingly well; make sure to lay the anchovy fillets directly on top of the tofu pieces. If you can't find the Japanese herb *mitsuba*, substitute 1 tablespoon coarsely chopped flat-leaf parsley.

Serves 4

VEGETABLE MARINADE

¼ cup red wine vinegar

2 cloves garlic, finely chopped

1 tablespoon soy sauce

¼ teaspoon freshly ground black pepper

½ teaspoon salt

5 tablespoons olive oil

SALAD

½ medium green bell pepper, cored, halved lengthwise, and sliced into 1-inch chunks

½ medium red bell pepper, cored, halved lengthwise, and sliced into 1-inch chunks

½ medium yellow bell pepper, cored, halved lengthwise, and sliced into 1-inch chunks

1 cup cherry tomatoes, stemmed and halved lengthwise

½ cup pitted black olives

¼ cup pickled pearl onions

½ package firm tofu (about ½ pound), cut into 24 even cubes

1 ounce anchovy fillets in oil, drained and cut into thirds

1 bunch mitsuba (about ⅛ cup), trimmed, leaves plucked, and stems coarsely chopped, for garnish

To make the marinade, whisk together all the ingredients in a large bowl. Add the bell peppers, tomatoes, olives, and pearl onions, tossing until all the ingredients are well coated. Add the tofu and gently toss to coat with the marinade, being careful not to break the tofu apart. Marinate the ingredients for 1 hour at room temperature.

Once the ingredients have marinated, transfer them to a platter. Scatter the anchovy pieces on top, especially over the tofu pieces. Sprinkle the *mitsuba* leaves and stems over the salad to garnish and serve.

SOURCES

GRILLING EQUIPMENT

These two Japanese kitchen equipment companies, both in New York City, carry outstanding Japanese *konro* and *shichirin* grills and traditional *binchotan* charcoal.

Korin Japanese Trading
New York, NY
Retail store; online store
www.korin.com

New York Mutual Trading
New York, NY
Retail store
www.japaneseculinary center.com

For American-style charcoal and gas grilling, we use Weber grills.
www.weber.com

JAPANESE INGREDIENTS

You can find ingredients for our recipes at Japanese, Korean, and Asian markets from coast to coast. The following is a list of Japanese supermarkets and markets online and across the country, plus a Korean supermarket chain that carries a wide selection of Japanese foods:

Online

Amazon
Search for ingredients in the "Grocery and Gourmet Food" section; they carry many Japanese ingredients (including *yuzu kosho*).
www.amazon.com

Asian Food Grocer
www.asianfoodgrocer.com

Mitsuwa
www.mitsuwa.com/english

National and Regional Chains

H-Mart
A Korean supermarket chain with stores nationwide. Check their website for the location nearest you.
www.hmart.com

Marukai
A California supermarket chain with eight locations around the state
www.marukai.com

Mitsuwa
A supermarket chain with locations in California, Illinois, and New Jersey
www.mitsuwa.com/english

Nijiya Market
A supermarket chain with locations in California, Hawaii, and New York
www.nijiya.com

California

Ebisu Supermarket
Fountain Valley
www.ocebisu.com

H Mart
Korean supermarket in Diamond Bar and Irvine
www.hmart.com

Maruka
Supermarket with eight locations in Northern and Southern California
www.marukai.com

Mitsuwa
Supermarket with six locations in Northern and Southern California
www.mitsuwa.com/english

Nijiya Market
Ten locations in Northern and Southern California
www.nijiya.com

Super Mira Market
San Francisco
(415) 921-6529

Tokyo Fish Market
Albany
(510) 524-7243

Colorado

H Mart
Korean supermarket in
Denver
www.hmart.com

Pacific Mercantile Company
Denver
www.pacificeastwest.com

Georgia

H Mart
Korean supermarket with
four locations
www.hmart.com

Illinois

H Mart
Korean supermarkets in
Niles and Naperville
www.hmart.com

Mitsuwa
Supermarket in
Arlington Heights
www.mitsuwa.com/english

Sea Ranch Grocery
Wilmette
(847) 256-7010

Tensuke Market
Elk Grove Village
www.tensuke.us

Maryland

Daruma Japanese Market
Bethesda
www.darumajapanmarket
.com

H Mart
Korean supermarket with
three locations
www.hmart.com

Massachusetts

Kotobukiya
Cambridge
www.kotobukiyamarket.com

Michigan

Koyama Shoten
Livonia
(734) 464-1480

One World Market
Novi
(248) 374-0844

New Jersey

Daido Market
Fort Lee
www.daidomarket.com

H Mart
Korean supermarket with four
locations
www.hmart.com

Mitsuwa
Supermarket in Edgewater
www.mitsuwa.com/english

New York

Daido Market
White Plains
www.daidomarket.com

Fuji Mart
Scarsdale
(914) 472-1510

H Mart
Korean supermarket with
five locations
www.hmart.com

JAS Mart
New York
(212) 866-4780

Katagiri
New York
www.katagiri.com

Nijiya Market
Hartsdale
www.nijiya.com

Sunrise Mart
New York; two locations
(212) 598-3040

Ohio

Tensuke Market
Columbus
www.tensukemarket.com

Oregon

H Mart
Korean supermarket in
Portland
www.hmart.com

Uwajimaya
Beaverton
www.uwajimaya.com

Pennsylvania

H Mart
Korean supermarket with
three locations
www.hmart.com

Maido
Narbeth
www.maidookini.com

Tokyo Japanese Store
Pittsburgh
www.tokyostorepgh.com

Texas

Daido Market
Houston
www.daidomarket.com

H Mart
Korean supermarket in
Carrollton and Houston
www.hmart.com

Shop Minoya
Plano
(972) 769-8346

Virginia

H Mart
Korean supermarket with
three locations
www.hmart.com

Naniwa Foods
McLean
(703) 893-7209

Washington

H Mart
Korean supermarket in Federal
Way and Lynnwood
www.hmart.com

Uwajimaya
Markets in Seattle and
Bellevue
www.uwajimaya.com

FINDING INGREDIENTS

IF YOU'RE NOT FAMILIAR WITH the ingredients in this book, navigating a Japanese market can be a challenge. To help make finding what you want easier, we've compiled this list of ingredients written out in both English and Japanese.

Bring this cookbook with you on your shopping trips to Japanese markets and reference this list—hopefully it will help you get what you need!

Soy sauce (*koikuchi*)
濃口しょうゆ

Mirin　みりん

Shiro miso　白みそ

Shinshu shiro miso
信州白みそ

Aka miso　赤みそ

Sendai miso　仙台みそ

Hatcho miso　八丁みそ

Aka dashi miso
赤だしみそ

Saikyo miso　西京みそ

Yuzu kosho　ゆずコショウ

Sea salt　自然海塩

Sesame oil　ごま 油

Sesame seed　ゴマ

Rice vinegar　米酢

Tobanjan　トウバンジャン

Wasabi　わさび

Karashi mustard　からし

Sansho　さんしょう

Shichimi togarashi
七 味とうがらし

Ume paste　ねり梅

Shiso　しそ

Yukari shiso salt　ゆかり塩

INDEX